# RELATED TITLES FOR COLLEGE-BOUND STUDENTS

The NEW SAT

The NEW SAT with CD-ROM

NEW SAT 2400

The NEW SAT Critical Reading Workbook

The NEW SAT Math Workbook

The NEW SAT Writing Workbook

## SAT II

SAT II Biology E/M

SAT II Chemistry

SAT II Literature

SAT II Math IC and IIC

SAT II Physics

SAT II Spanish

SAT II U.S. History

SAT II World History

## Vocabulary-Building for the SAT

Extreme SAT Vocabulary Flashcards Flip-O-Matic

SAT Vocabulary Flashcards Flip-O-Matic

SAT Vocab Velocity

Frankenstein: A Kaplan SAT Score-Raising Classic

The Ring of McAllister: A Score-Raising Mystery Featuring
1,046 Must-Know SAT Vocabulary Words

## SAT for Native Spanish Speakers

Domina el SAT: Prepárate para Tomar el Examen para Ingresar a la Universidad

**Test Prep and Admissions**

# Inside the
# NEW SAT

## 10 Strategies To Help You
## Score Higher

By the Staff of Kaplan Test Prep and Admissions

**Simon & Schuster**

NEW YORK · LONDON · SYDNEY · TORONTO

Kaplan Publishing
Published by Simon & Schuster
1230 Avenue of the Americas
New York, NY 10020

Contributing Editors: Seppy Basili and Jon Zeitlin

Production Manager: Michael Shevlin

Executive Editor: Jennifer Farthing

June 2004

10 9 8 7 6 5 4 3 2 1

Manufactured in the United States of America
Published simultaneously in Canada

ISBN 0-7432-6496-7

# Table of Contents

### kaptest.com/booksonline

As an owner of this guide, you are entitled to get more SAT practice and help online. Log on to **kaptest.com/booksonline** to access vocabulary flashcards and additional practice quizzes.

Access to this selection of Kaplan's online SAT practice questions is free of charge to purchasers of this book. When you log on, you'll be asked to input the book's ISBN number (see the bar code on the back cover). And you'll be asked for a specific password derived from a passage in this book, so have your book handy when you log on.

### kaptest.com/publishing

The material in this book is up to date at the time of publication. However, since the New SAT does not debut until March 2005, certain details are not yet public. The College Entrance Examination Board may institute changes in the test after this book goes to print. For any important late-breaking developments—or changes or corrections to the Kaplan test preparation materials in this book—go to **kaptest.com/publishing**.

### kaplansurveys.com/books

What did you think of this book? We'd love to hear your comments and suggestions. We invite you to fill out our online survey form at **kaplansurveys.com/books**. Your feedback is extremely helpful as we continue to develop high-quality resources to meet your needs.

**Note:** At the time of printing, the precise number of questions for the New SAT had not been released by the College Entrance Examination Board. Use the practice quizzes and writing prompts in chapters 3–9 to help you gauge your strengths and weaknesses accurately.

# Introduction

The SAT has undergone the biggest facelift in its entire history. But don't be scared—be relieved. Why? Because we know what's on the new SAT, and we know exactly how you should prepare for it.

Kaplan has been teaching kids how to attack the SAT for over 65 years—longer than anyone else, period. *Inside the NEW SAT* takes time-tested strategies from our SAT prep books and courses and couples them with brand new strategies for the brand new parts of the SAT. Things like:

- How to write a killer SAT essay
- How to attack the SAT's new, harder math
- How to manage your time on test day
- How to improve your SAT vocabulary, fast
- When to guess, and when to move on

We give you all this and much, much more in a manageable, easy-to-read book that includes over 100 practice questions.

Every strategy and practice question in this book is geared to do one thing—get you more points on the new SAT. If you learn just one of the strategies in this book, your score should improve. And, if you apply them all? Then the new SAT will cower in your very presence.

So don't freak out over the new SAT—Kaplan's got you covered.

# How to Use *Inside the NEW SAT*

This book is designed to be as user-friendly as possible. You can read it from front to back; from back to front—however you want. All we ask is that you read chapter 1 first—it's an overview of the changes and format of the new SAT. After that, it's up to you.

Each chapter of *Inside the NEW SAT* is designed as a separate, stand-alone unit. Each chapter helps you understand an important aspect of scoring well on the new SAT, whether it be how to write a great SAT essay or how to build your vocabulary before test day.

Each chapter uses a mix of strategies, tips, explanations, and practice questions to prepare your brain for the teasing it is about to endure. Here are a few tips to make *Inside the NEW SAT* an even more powerful tool in your quest for a higher score:

- Pay special attention to Kaplan's "Attack Strategies." These are step-by-step approaches to specific SAT question types. We alert you to Kaplan's Attack Strategy like this:

- Do all of the practice questions. There are about 100 of them. Answering the questions is really important because it reinforces the material you just covered.

- Practice writing the essay by using our writing prompts in chapter 3. You'll quickly learn that writing a good SAT essay is nothing to worry about.

- Read the "Remember..." summaries at the end of every chapter. If you are still uneasy about anything in the summary, go back and review it.

Good luck, friend.

# Chapter One: **What's New about the New SAT**

- **New Writing Section**
- **Changes to the Critical Reading Section**
- **Changes to the Math Section**
- **Changes to Your Score**

The SAT has gotten a major facelift. Beginning with the March 2005 administration, the SAT is a little longer, a little harder, and a lot different. There are changes in the content tested and the types of questions used, all starting in March 2005. Here are the most important changes. (All of the SAT's new content and changes to the old content will be covered in detail in later chapters.)

## CHANGES ON THE NEW SAT

### The New Writing Component

The biggest change in the SAT is the addition of a writing section to the test. The writing test has two parts: a multiple-choice section and a written essay. The multiple-choice questions test your ability to identify sentence errors and to make improvements in sentences and paragraphs. The essay section tests your writing ability.

### Changes to the "Verbal" Section

For years and years, the SAT had a part called the Verbal section. Not anymore. Now it's called the Critical Reading section. How is it different? The old SAT's Analogies section (*old* is to *young* as *Madonna* is to ... ?) is history. In place of these Analogies are new, short reading passages followed by multiple-choice questions. (The regular reading passages and questions are still on the test, and so are the sentence completion questions.)

## Changes to the Math Section

Some harder questions are being added to the SAT Math section. These questions cover the math usually taught in high school algebra II classes. In addition, the old Quantitative Comparison questions, which required a comparison of a quantity in column A to a quantity in column B, have gotten the axe. They have been replaced with multiple-choice questions and Grid-in questions (A.K.A. "student-produced responses") that test the more difficult math.

### EXPERIMENTAL SECTION

Every SAT has an experimental section. The experimental section is used by the test makers to try out new questions before they use them in upcoming SATs. The experimental section does not count in your score. It can show up anywhere on the exam and will look like just like a normal section. DO NOT try to figure out which SAT section is experimental. You will fail to do so. Treat all the sections as if they count.

## Scoring the New Test

The new Writing test is scored on a scale of 200–800, as are the Math and Critical Reading sections. So the composite scores on the new test are 600–2400, instead of the 400–1600 on the old SAT. That means a 1600 is no longer a perfect score—a 2400 is. (One benefit: If you get a 1600 on the new test, and you tell an old person you got a 1600 on the SAT, the old person will think you are a genius.)

## SAT Test Dates

Because of all these changes, more students are taking the SAT earlier. There are two reasons for this:

- More students are applying to early decision programs.
- More students are taking the SAT more than once.

As a general rule, it's important to get SAT scores under your belt by the end of your junior year. That way you know where you stand as you plan your college choices. Plus, it's likely that you'll improve your score by taking the exam again, since it will be familiar to you.

The SAT is administered on select Saturdays during the school year. Sunday testing is available for students who cannot take the Saturday test because of religious observances. Here are the upcoming dates for the new SAT in 2005:

| Test Date | Registration Deadlines U.S. and International | U.S. Late Registration Deadlines |
|---|---|---|
| March 12, 2005 | February 7, 2005 | February 16, 2005 |
| May 7, 2005 | March 25, 2005 | April 6, 2005 |
| June 4, 2005 | April 29, 2005 | May 11, 2005 |

## SAT REGISTRATION

Check the College Board website at www.collegeboard.com for complete information about registering for the SAT. Here are some important highlights.

- To register for the SAT by mail, you'll need to get a Registration Bulletin from your high school guidance counselor.
- You can register online at www.collegeboard.com/sat/html/satform.html. *Important:* Not all students are eligible to register online, so read the instructions and requirements *carefully*.
- Register early to secure the time you want at the test center of your choice and to avoid late registration fees.
- Students with Disabilities can call (609) 771-7137 (TTY: (609) 882-4118) for more information.
- At press time, the basic fee is about $40 in the United States. This price includes reports for you, your high school, and up to four colleges and scholarship programs.
- You may reregister by telephone if you've previously registered for the SAT and you require no special forms (like a fee waiver). If you have a touch-tone phone and a major credit card, you can reregister by calling (800) SAT-SCORE.

- You will receive an admission ticket at least a week before the test. The ticket confirms your registration at a specified date, at a specified test center. Make sure to bring it, and proper identification, with you to the test center. Some acceptable forms of identification include photo IDs such as a driver's license, a school identification card, and a valid passport. (*Unacceptable* forms of identification include a social security card, credit card, and birth certificate.)

- SAT scores will be available online approximately three weeks after the test. If you can't wait that long, you can get your scores eight days earlier with Scores by Web or Scores by Phone. Please visit www.collegeboard.com for more information.

- Remember to check with the College Board for all the latest information on the new SAT. Every effort has been made to keep the information in this book as up-to-date as possible, but changes may occur after the book is published.

- Finally, bookmark the College Board's website: www.collegeboard.com.

## HOW THE NEW SAT IS STRUCTURED

The new SAT is three hours and forty-five minutes long. It is a mostly multiple-choice exam, with a written essay and some student-produced math as the exceptions. It's divided into eight sections: three Math, three Critical Reading, and two Writing sections. They can appear in any order on test day. There are two ten-minute breaks.

The sections are broken down like this:

### SAT Section Breakdowns

| Section | Length | Content | Type |
|---|---|---|---|
| 1. Critical Reading | 25 minutes | Sentence Completion and Reading Comprehension questions | Multiple-choice |
| 2. Critical Reading | 25 minutes | Sentence Completion and Reading Comprehension questions | Multiple-choice |
| 3. Critical Reading | 20 minutes | Sentence Completion and Reading Comprehension questions | Multiple-choice |
| 4. Math | 25 minutes | High school Geometry and Algebra, Number and Operations, Statistics, Probability, and Data Analysis | Multiple-choice and student-produced responses |

| 5. | Math | 25 minutes | High school Geometry and Algebra, Number and Operations, Statistics, Probability, and Data Analysis | Multiple-choice and student-produced responses |
|---|---|---|---|---|
| 6. | Math | 20 minutes | High school Geometry and Algebra, Number and Operations, Statistics, Probability, and Data Analysis | Multiple-choice and student-produced responses |
| 7. | Writing | 25 minutes | Student-written essay | Long-form essay |
| 8. | Writing | 35 minutes | Usage, Sentence Corrections, and Paragraph Correction questions | Multiple-choice |
| 9. | Experimental | 25 minutes | Math, Writing, or Critical Reading | (Anything goes—depending on content, this may be multiple-choice or student-produced) |

## WRITING COMPONENT

This is the big new component on the SAT. It is made up of two sections that test your writing skills: a written essay, and a set of multiple-choice questions on writing topics.

### The Essay

The Essay asks you to write a persuasive essay on a given topic, like this one:

**Directions:** Consider carefully the following statement(s) and the assignment below it.

"The happiness of a man in this life does not consist in the absence but in the mastery of his passions."

—Alfred Lord Tennyson

**Assignment:** Is there a time when you controlled your emotions and things turned out for the better? In an essay, support your position using an example (or examples) from literature, the arts, science and technology, current events or your own experience or observation.

## Multiple-Choice Questions

The Writing component's multiple-choice questions test your ability to spot grammar mistakes, mistakes in sentence structure, and mistakes in paragraph structure (how sentences work together). Here's an example of a sentence structure question:

> By the time I graduate from college three years from now, my brother <u>has practiced</u> law for five years.
>
> (A) has practiced
>
> (B) has been practicing
>
> (C) will have been practicing
>
> (D) would have practiced
>
> (E) is practicing          [Answer: C]

## CRITICAL READING COMPONENT

There are two kinds of questions on the Critical Reading component of the SAT. They are both multiple-choice questions.

## Sentence Completion Questions

These questions test your ability to see how the parts of a sentence relate. From what we've heard, about half of the questions have one word missing from a sentence; the other half may have two words missing. Both types test vocabulary and reasoning skills.

Here is a sample question:

> The queen's - - - - decisions as a diplomat and administrator led to her legendary reputation as a just and - - - - ruler.
>
> (A) quick . . capricious
>
> (B) equitable . . wise
>
> (C) immoral . . perceptive
>
> (D) generous . . witty
>
> (E) clever . . uneducated          [Answer: B]

Sentence Completion questions have always been arranged by order of difficulty on the SAT, and we don't think this will change now. The first few questions in a set are meant to be fairly easy. The middle few questions will be a little harder, and the last few are the most difficult. Keep this in mind as you work.

## Reading Comprehension Questions

These questions test your ability to understand a piece of writing. The passages are short (about 100–150 words) and long (about 400–850 words), and at least one passage contains two related readings. Most Critical Reading questions test how well you understand the passage, some ask you to draw conclusions, and some test your vocabulary.

Here is a sample vocabulary question. It would appear on the test after one of the above-mentioned reading passages:

> As used in the passage, *unmatched* (line 27)
> most nearly means
>
> (A) uneven
>
> (B) solitary
>
> (C) outmoded
>
> (D) noncompeting
>
> (E) supreme

Reading Comprehension questions are not arranged by difficulty. Whenever you find yourself spending too much time on a Reading Comprehension question, you should skip it and return to it later.

### SAT GROUND RULES

These are rules you can use to your advantage. Not knowing these rules can lead to major time management snafus…and a lower score.

- You are NOT allowed to jump back and forth between sections.
- You are NOT allowed to return to earlier sections to change answers.
- You are NOT allowed to spend more than the allotted time on any section.
- You CAN move around within a section.
- You CAN flip through your section at the beginning to see what type of questions are coming up.

## MATH COMPONENT

There are two kinds of questions on the Math component, broken down like so:

### Regular Math

These questions are straightforward multiple-choice math questions, with five answer choices.

Some of the concepts likely to be tested on the new SAT include*:

**Basic Math**
Remainders
Averages
Ratios
Rates
Percents
Combinations
Simultaneous equations
Symbols
Special triangles
Multiple and strange figures

**Advanced Math**
Sequences
Sets
Absolute value
Rational equations and inequalities
Radical equations
Integers and rational exponents
Direct and inverse variation

Function notation and evaluation
Domain and range
Functions as models
Linear functions—equations and graphs
Quadratic functions—equations and graphs
Geometric notation
Problems in which trigonometry can be used as an alternative method of solution
Properties of tangent lines
Coordinate geometry
Qualitative behavior of graphs and functions
Transformations and their effect on graphs and functions
Data interpretation, scatterplots, and matrices
Geometric probability

*This list isn't meant to be comprehensive; these are just SOME of the concepts that have been tested a lot (10 basic math) and SOME of the things Kaplan thinks will be tested (20 advanced math).

Here is a sample question:

> If $x + y = 8$ and $y - x = -2$, then $y =$
>
> (A) $-2$
>
> (B) $3$
>
> (C) $5$
>
> (D) $8$
>
> (E) $10$                                                    [Answer: B]

## Grid-ins

Grid-ins are not multiple-choice questions. Instead of picking an answer choice, you write your response in a little grid like this:

Here is a sample Grid-in question:

> A retailer buys 16 shirts at $4.50 each, and she
> sells all 16 shirts for $6.75 each. If the retailer
> purchases more of these shirts at $4.50 each,
> what is the greatest number of these shirts
> that she can buy with the profit she made on
> the 16 shirts?
>
>                                                    [Answer: 8]

Both question types cover the same math concepts. Either one can ask you a geometry, algebra, or statistics question. The only difference is that one asks you to write your answer, the other asks you to fill in a bubble. Actually, there is *another* big difference in the two types of questions, and that has to do with how a wrong answer is scored.

## HOW THE NEW SAT IS SCORED

You gain one point for each correct answer on the SAT and lose a FRACTION of a point for each wrong answer. You do not gain or lose any points for questions you leave blank.

The only exception is with Grid-ins, where you lose *nothing* for a wrong answer. That's why you must always fill in an answer on the Grid-ins—you have absolutely, positively nothing to lose.

The totals for the Writing, Critical Reading, and Math sections are added up to produce three raw scores. These raw scores are then converted into scaled scores, with 200 as the lowest score and 800 the highest.

Knowing how the new SAT works is key to doing well on the test. You don't want any surprises on test day. So now that you know what to expect on the new SAT, let's get to chapter 2—Kaplan's 10 Must-Have Strategies for getting your highest score possible.

# REMEMBER...

The SAT is divided into nine sections:

- 3 Critical Reading sections
- 3 Math sections
- 2 Writing sections
- 1 Experimental section

Some sections (but not all) arrange their questions from easiest to hardest.

You gain 1 point for every question you get right; you lose no points for leaving a blank.

You lose a fraction of a point for every question you get wrong (except for Grid-ins).

# Chapter Two: **Kaplan's 10 Must-Have Strategies**

- **The New SAT Is Not Like Other Tests**
- **7 Basic SAT Strategies**
- **3 Time Management Strategies**

When you take a test at school, you probably approach it something like this:

- You go through the problems in order.
- You spend more time on the hard questions than on easy ones, since harder questions are usually worth more points.
- You often show your work, since many teachers give credit if you do most of the work right, even if you get the answer wrong.

None of these strategies work on the SAT. If you approach the SAT this way, your score will suffer. On the SAT:

- You benefit from moving around within a section.
- The hard questions are worth the same as the easy ones.
- It doesn't matter how you answer the question—all that matters is picking the right answer.

## THE NEW SAT—IT'S NOT LIKE OTHER TESTS

Why are we making such a big deal about this right up front? Because you can use this knowledge—and other basic strategies—to gain lots of points on the SAT. By using the strategies that follow, you don't need to learn a single vocabulary word or math concept to improve your SAT score.

We've divided the 10 Must-Have Strategies into two types: *basic*, or general best practices for conquering the SAT, and *time management*, or techniques that will keep you on target for a high score.

## BASIC TEST-TAKING STRATEGIES

When it comes to the SAT, follow our seven proven test-taking strategies to pick up quick points, to guess smarter, and to prevent careless mistakes.

## STRATEGY 1: KNOW THE DIRECTIONS IN ADVANCE

One of the easiest things you can do to help your performance on the SAT is to understand the directions before taking the test. Since the directions are always exactly the same, there's no reason to waste your time on the day of the test reading them. Tackle them now.

We provide sample SAT directions for all of the SAT sections in the chapters that follow. Make sure you learn them as you go through this book so you don't have to waste time reading them during the test. On test day, eight sets of directions could take you eight minutes to read. Let's say you answer just *one* extra question right for every *two* minutes you save skipping the directions. That's 4–5 more points—just from knowing the directions in advance.

---

### IMPORTANT EXCEPTION: READ THE WRITING DIRECTIONS

There is one thing we want to make perfectly clear. Remember, this is the NEW SAT, so there are some new instructions that nobody except the test creators has actually seen: the Writing section directions. We've found out what you're expected to do--and we show you how to go about doing it in chapter 3--but we don't necessarily have the exact wording that the SAT will use. So, just to be on the safe side, we recommend that you read those directions during the test.

## STRATEGY 2: DON'T ANSWER QUESTIONS IN ORDER

You're allowed to skip around within each section of the SAT. High scorers know this. They move through the test efficiently. They don't waste time on any one question, even a hard one, until they've tried every question at least once. Remember, easy questions are worth the same points as harder questions.

When you run into a question that looks tough, circle it in your test booklet and skip it. Go back and try again after you have answered the easier ones. If you get two easy ones right in the time it would have taken you to get one harder one right, you just gained points.

There's another benefit to coming back to harder questions later. On a second look, scary questions can turn out to be simple. By answering some easier questions first, you can come back to a harder question with fresh eyes and a little more confidence.

## STRATEGY 3: KNOW WHEN TO GUESS

There is no penalty for guessing on the SAT. There is only a penalty for guessing *wrong*. If you can eliminate one or more answers that are definitely incorrectly, you'll turn the odds in your favor and *come out ahead* by guessing.

Here's why. If you get an answer wrong on any multiple-choice question on the SAT, you lose 1/4 point. The fractional points you lose are supposed to offset the points you might get "accidentally" by guessing the correct answer. By learning Kaplan's techniques, you can eliminate a few answer choices on most questions, even if you have no idea what the right answer is. By learning how to eliminate wrong answer choices, you can actually turn the guessing "penalty" to your advantage.

Let's take a close look at this, to make sure you are confident with this strategy. By eliminating one wrong answer in five, you are down to four answer choices. So you have a 1 in 4 chance of guessing correctly. So, for every four questions you answer, you should get something like 1 right and 3 wrong. 1 right = 1 point. 3 wrong = 3/4 points.

$$1 - 3/4 = 1/4 \text{ point}$$

So, by eliminating just one answer choice and guessing on four questions, you have gained 1/4 point! This may not seem like a lot, but over the course of a long test, these fractions really add up, and can increase your score significantly. And, of course, if you can eliminate two or three wrong answers, your chances—and score—improve even more.

## STRATEGY 4: ANSWER ALL GRID-INS

If you get an answer wrong on a Grid-in Math question, you lose nothing. So you MUST write in an answer for every Grid-in. The worst that can happen is that you get zero points on the questions you guessed on. If you get just one right, that's an extra point to add to the 4–5 points you already got by skipping the directions. Add up a couple of fractions, and you've already increased your raw score—and you've only learned four strategies so far!

## STRATEGY 5: FILL OUT YOUR ANSWER SHEET THE RIGHT WAY

When time is short, it's easy to get confused going back and forth between your test book and the big sheet of bubbles. If you know the answer but fill in the wrong answer bubble, you won't get the points. To avoid mistakes on the answer grid, follow these steps.

### Circle the Questions You Skip

Put a circle in your test book around any question numbers you skip. When you go back, these questions will be easy to locate. Also, if you accidentally skip a box on the grid, you can quickly check your grid against your book to see where you went wrong.

Perhaps the most common SAT disaster is filling in all of the questions with the right answers—in the wrong spots. To avoid this sad fate, every time you skip a question, circle it in your test book, then make doubly sure that you skip it on the answer grid as well.

### Circle Your Answer in Your Test Book

Circling your answers in the test book makes it easier to check your grid against your book. It also makes the next grid strategy possible.

## Grid Five or More Answers at Once

Don't transfer your answers to the grid after every question. Transfer your answers after every five questions, or at the end of each reading passage. That way, you won't keep breaking your concentration to mark the grid. You'll save time and you'll gain accuracy.

## Keep Track of Time

You need to be mindful of the time remaining toward the end of each section—time may be running out! You don't want to have your answers in the test booklet and not be able to transfer them to your answer grid because you have run out of time. Remember, questions answered correctly in the test booklet get you zero points. All that matters is what's on the answer sheet at the end of the exam.

## STRATEGY 6: READ THE QUESTION CAREFULLY BEFORE YOU LOOK AT THE ANSWER

The people who make the test love to put distractors among the answer choices. Distractors are answer choices that look like the right answer, but aren't. If you jump right into the answer choices without pausing to think first about what you're looking for, you're much more likely to fall for one of these traps.

## STRATEGY 7: WRITE YOUR ESSAY

If you "guess" on the essay section and write a terrible essay, you get 1 "raw point," no matter how bad it was. (We'll go into essay scoring in detail later.) If you freeze and skip the essay, you get zero. The essay is worth 1/3 of your total 800-point Writing score. So try to write a great essay, but if you freeze up under pressure, at least manage to get something down that responds to the writing prompt.

## TIME MANAGEMENT STRATEGIES

The SAT is three hours and forty-five minutes long. You are going to answer a lot of questions in that period of time. So managing your time is extremely important to your score. That's why we have three specific time management strategies you need to use when you take the SAT.

## STRATEGY 8: USE THE SAT'S "ORDER OF DIFFICULTY"

Most sections arrange their questions from easiest to hardest, but some don't. This is extremely important, because the strategies for the sections depend on the order of difficulty (or lack thereof). So here's the rundown.

| Order of Difficulty* | Easiest > Hardest |
| --- | --- |
| Critical Reading Component: Sentence Completions | Y |
| Critical Reading Component: Reading Comprehension | N |
| All Math Sections | Y |
| Writing Component: Multiple Choice | Y |
| Writing Component: Essay | N/A |

As you work through a section that orders its questions from easiest to hardest, always be aware of where you are in the set. When working on the easy problems, you can generally trust your first impulse—the obvious answer is likely to be right. As you get to the end of the set, you need to become more suspicious. The answers probably *shouldn't* come easily. If they do, look at the problem again, because the obvious answer is likely to be wrong. (We go into detail on several tricks the SAT uses to trip you up on math questions in chapter 7.)

## STRATEGY 9: LOCATE QUICK POINTS IF YOU'RE RUNNING OUT OF TIME

Some questions can be done quickly. For instance, some reading comprehension questions will ask you to identify the meaning of a particular word in the passage. These can be done at the last minute, even if you haven't read the passage. When you start to run out of time, locate and answer any of the quick points that remain. When you take the SAT, you have one clear objective in mind—to score as many points as you can. It's that simple.

* Based on previous SATs

---

**WRITE YOUR ESSAY THEM MOVE ON TO
THE MULTIPLE-CHOICE QUESTIONS**

The essay section is 25 minutes long. The multiple-choice section is 35 minutes long. The essay is administered first, followed directly by the multiple-choice questions. If you finish the essay in less than 25 minutes, you may move right into the multiple-choice questions.

## STRATEGY 10: DO SCs FIRST, SHORT RCs SECOND, AND LONG RCs LAST

We're talking Critical Reading here. You can earn points faster on Sentence Completion questions, so you should do these first. You should do Sentence Completion questions first even if they are the last questions in a section.

Next, do the Reading Comprehension questions based on short passages. Why? It takes less time to read a short passage then it does to read a long one, so the short passage points are faster.

Do the questions linked to long passages in the time remaining. This is very important! You *do not* want to get bogged down in long passages and leave yourself just a few minutes for short passages and sentence completion questions. And leave the paired passage set (the one that uses two passages instead of one) for last, because this is the most time-consuming passage of all.

## REMEMBER...

You need to use the SAT's unique structure to your advantage. Be familiar with every section, question type, and answer type in the SAT. Here are the 10 strategies for conquering the SAT:

1. Know the directions so you don't have to read them on test day.

2. Don't answer questions in order–skip around within sections.

3. Guess when you can rule out at least one answer choice.

4. Answer all Grid-In questions (because you don't lose any points for wrong answers).

5. Fill in your answer sheet the smart way.

6. Write your essay, even if you think it's going to be bad.

7. Read questions carefully before you answer.

8. Know how to find fast points when you are running out of time.

9. If you finish your essay early, move on to the multiple-choice questions.

10. Do Sentence Completion questions first in the Critical Reading sections.

# Chapter Three: **How to Write a High-Scoring SAT Essay**

- **The New Essay Component**
- **Kaplan's SAT Essay Attack Strategy**
- **Model Essays**

The new SAT has a new Writing section. The new Writing section has two parts, one of which is a student-written essay. To score well on the SAT essay, you need to write a short, persuasive essay on an assigned topic.

The word *persuasive* here is key. You could write the best essay ever on the pros and cons of wearing sensible shoes, but if you have not persuaded the reader into seeing things from your point of view (either pro sensible shoes or con), you won't get a high score.

You don't need any specific knowledge to complete the SAT essay. So don't "study" for it by reading newspapers, magazines, or encyclopedias. The essay will be on a general topic, so you'll be able to write about what you know and are interested in.

## THE NEW WRITING SECTION: ESSAY

There are two kinds of SAT essay prompts—a "one-quote" essay and a "two-quote" essay. Here is an example of each, so you can see what we mean:

## "ONE-QUOTE" ESSAY

**Directions:** Consider carefully the following statement(s) and the assignment below it.

> "A sense of humor is part of the art of leadership, of getting along with people, of getting things done."
>
> —President Dwight D. Eisenhower

**Assignment:** It is important for the president of the United States to have a theory on leadership qualities. Is it important for a high school student to have formulated such a theory? Why or why not? In an essay, support your position by discussing an example (or examples) from literature, science and technology, the arts, current events, or your own experience or observation.

## "TWO-QUOTE" ESSAY

**Directions:** Consider carefully the following statement(s) and the assignment below it.

> "Boredom, not will, is the mother of change."
>
> —Mason Cooley, *British Novelists Since 1900*

> "If you don't like something, change it. If you can't change it, change your attitude. Don't complain."
>
> —Maya Angelou, *Open Wide the Freedom Gates*

**Assignment:** Is change motivated more often by a specific goal, or by boredom with what you have? The quotations above give two opinions. Plan and write an essay detailing your view on this question. (Remember that change can happen on different levels, from internal revelations to social revolutions.) In an essay, support your position by discussing an example (or examples) from literature, science and technology, the arts, current events, or your own experience or observation.

## ESSAY SCORING

Your essay is scored on a scale of 1–6. It is scored by two judges. Here is how your essay will be graded:

| Score | Demonstrates | Organization | Language |
|-------|-------------|--------------|----------|
| 6 | clear and consistent competence, though it may have errors | is well organized and fully developed with supporting examples | displays consistent language facility, varied sentence structure, and range of vocabulary |
| 5 | reasonable competence, with occasional errors or lapses in quality | is generally organized and well developed with appropriate examples | displays language facility, with syntactic variety and a range of vocabulary |
| 4 | adequate competence with occasional errors and lapses in quality | is organized and adequately developed with examples | displays adequate but inconsistent language facility |
| 3 | developing competence, with weaknesses | inadequate organization or development | many errors in grammar or diction; little variety |
| 2 | some incompetence with one or more weaknesses | poor organization, thin development | frequent errors in grammar and diction; no variety |
| 1 | incompetence, with serious flaws | no organization, no development | severe grammar and diction errors obscure meaning |

A score of 0 will be given to an essay not written on the given topic.

Here are Kaplan's three strategies for writing a solid SAT essay.

## ESSAY STRATEGY 1: WRITE THE RIGHT-LENGTH ESSAY

SAT essays that get high scores (in the 10–12 range when both judges' scores are combined) are generally longer than essays with lower scores. In fact, essays in the 10–12 range are ALWAYS at least three to five paragraphs long, and each of those paragraphs ALMOST ALWAYS contains more than two sentences.

So you need to write an essay that has three-to-five paragraphs, with each paragraph containing more than two sentences. One or two paragraphs, no matter how well-written, will not get you a 10 or a 12, and that's what you're shooting for.

## ESSAY STRATEGY 2: DON'T WRITE JUST ABOUT PERSONAL HISTORY, IF POSSIBLE

Essay topics are so broad that you can always steer your essay toward a subject that you are familiar with. Just make sure you:

- Address the topic that you are given, and
- Write persuasively.

The object is to convince your reader to see something from your point of view. Don't worry about what the reader thinks—write about what *you* think. You are NOT fair and balanced! (Well, you should be fair, but definitely not balanced.)

Then, if the topic allows, it's a good idea to include references to current events, history, and literature in your essay. Now, you don't *have* to use these things as examples. You could also just use your personal experience. But if the essay topic allows it, and you have a good example from history, famous books, or the nightly news, please include it.

Why? Your essay is being graded by high school teachers and college professors. You know teachers—they want to know that the things they have taught you are sinking in. They'll be impressed by an essay that goes beyond your personal experience. But if you don't have any such supporting evdience from the outside world, don't force it. Go with what you know.

## ESSAY STRATEGY 3: BE NEAT

Your essay must be readable. If you edit what you've written, do it neatly. If you add a word, change a phrase, or cross out a sentence, do it carefully. It may sound silly, but neatness matters. It matters a lot.

Why? The graders have tons of essays to read and grade. That means they don't spend much time reading your essay (about a minute, on average). They aren't going to read an essay three or four times in order to decipher hard-to-read words or sentences. They are going to read it once, score it, and move on. Make life easier for them by writing neatly, and they'll be more inclined to make life easier for you.

To sum up: You're not expected to produce a perfect piece of writing. The graders know that you have only 25 minutes to think about, write, and proofread your work. What they expect is an organized and readable piece of writing that makes an argument supported by real examples. The rest of this chapter will show you how to accomplish this goal.

## WRITE A HIGH-SCORING SAT ESSAY

Each essay section uses one or two quotations to set up its question. This is called the "essay prompt." You answer the essay prompt with a 3–5 paragraph, neat, persuasive essay, as we just described.

Sometimes an essay prompt uses one quotation, sometimes it uses two. You won't know which it will be until you open your SAT. The quotations can be long or short. Either way, they do one thing: set up a topic for you to write about. Remember, you must write on the topic provided; if you don't you could get a zero. The quotes will almost always be upbeat, but that doesn't mean your essay has to be. Your essay can take the opposing view, or go in any direction you want, but the prompt itself will likely be, in some measure, life affirming.

Here's another example of an SAT essay prompt.

> **Directions:** Consider carefully the following statement(s) and the assignment below it.
>
> > "If there were in the world today any large number of people who desired the happiness of others more than they desired their own happiness, we could have paradise in a few years."
> >
> > —Bertrand Faberge
>
> **Assignment:** Is the "paradise" the writer mentions something that you think is possible, considering your own views on human nature? In an essay, support your position by discussing an example (or examples) from literature, science and technology, the arts, current events, or your own experience or observation.

## KAPLAN'S ESSAY ATTACK STRATEGY

So now you know what kind of essay prompt you can expect to see on the SAT. Kaplan has a great attack strategy for writing the essay. After you read the essay prompt, you:

**T** HINK about the topic (2 minutes)

**O** RGANIZE your paragraphs (5 minutes)

**W** RITE your essay (15 minutes)

**F** IX any mistakes (3 minutes)

We know what you're thinking: Wait, I don't start writing for seven minutes? This test is long and hard! Every minute counts! You are right. Every minute does count, so you need to use your minutes the *right* way. Here's our minute-by-minute rundown of the "TOWF" method.

### Minutes 1–2: Think

This step takes two minutes. That leaves you 23 minutes to outline, write, and fix your essay. Do NOT write anything during these two minutes. There's plenty of time for that later. Use these precious 120 seconds for thinking, and nothing else.

Read the topic statement and assignment carefully. The topic statement is going to be very broad. To narrow it down, you need to come up with an argument that specifically addresses the topic.

Let's say that you get the prompt from our sample essay question:

> Is the "paradise" the writer mentions something that you think is possible, considering your own views of human nature?

You need to take a specific example or examples from your personal experience, current events, history, literature, or any other discipline, and use these examples to compose an essay that answers this statement persuasively, one way or the other.

## Pick a Side

Decide either to agree or disagree with the topic statement. For example, you might "agree" with the statement by saying that this paradise is something that's possible, or you might "disagree" by saying you do not think it is possible. You do not want to say that you can kind of see things from both sides, even if that is, in fact, the case. If you're not sure what you think, pick the side you think you can best back up with examples.

## Choose Your Examples

Once you have picked your side, you must choose examples that back up your argument. Think of 2–3 examples that you can write about intelligently and passionately. Let's agree that this paradise is possible. Here are some possible examples to back up your opinion:

> Is the "paradise" the writer mentions something that you think is possible, considering your own views of human nature?

YES—human nature is good and generous

1. Regular people volunteer to help the less fortunate all the time.

2. Bono is always helping to fight hunger and he makes a big difference, and he's just one guy

3. The United States sends aid to poor countries

Once you have your examples, organize them in a way you think would flow best from paragraph to paragraph. You can do this by numbering your examples, as we did.

### Use Specific Evidence

You've got to cite evidence to support your examples. When you are thinking of your examples, also be thinking about one piece of evidence for each of your examples. Like so:

1. Regular people volunteer to help the less fortunate all the time.

   EXAMPLE: My sister spends every Sunday morning at the soup kitchen downtown.

2. Bono is always helping to fight hunger and he makes a big difference, and he's just one guy

   EXAMPLE: U2's lead singer went on a tour with the former U.S. Secretary of the Treasury to Africa and got him to admit there's a huge problem with starvation there and the United States needs to do something about it.

3. The United States sends aid to poor countries

   EXAMPLE: Congress just passed over $100 million in aid to drill for potable water in famine-struck African villages.

### Minutes 3–7: Organize

This step takes up to five minutes. That may seem like a lot of time to spend before your write a single essay sentence. But taking a few minutes to organize your essay is definitely worth the time. If you take a few minutes to outline what you want to write, the essay will be a lot easier to write once you start it. The time you take organizing will reduce the time it takes to write your essay.

So you have your argument, your examples, and your evidence in your head. It's time to plan your essay. Use the margins on your test booklet to outline your ideas. Here is how your essay paragraphs should be organized:

**Paragraph 1:**
- Clearly state your argument.
- Briefly mention the evidence that you're going to cite in support of that argument.

**Middle Paragraphs (2–3 paragraphs):**
- Explore and explain your evidence in detail. These paragraphs explain how the evidence supports the argument.

**Last Paragraph:**
- Briefly summarize your argument.

So, sticking with "people are good/paradise is possible," an outline might look like this:

P1. I think paradise is possible, because there are a bunch of people who are kind and generous. For example my sister, Bono, and the aid the United States gives to poor countries.

P2. My sister is a freshman in high school. She is on the soccer team, has a part-time job, and helps out with chores at home. She is very busy. But she still finds time every Sunday to help at the YMCA soup kitchen downtown.

P3. My sister is young but that doesn't mean one person can't do a lot. Bono went on a tour of Africa with Paul O'Neil in 2002. O'Neil was skeptical, but Bono proved to him that we could help.

P4. U.S. Congress approved over $100 million for drilling extra deep wells in villages in Africa. Where does that money come from? From all of us. We're all helping.

P5. In conclusion, my sister, Bono, and this country's elected officials and taxpayers, prove that human nature is good, and that we can all work to get closer to the paradise the writer talks about.

## Minutes 8–22: Write

So what's left? Writing your high-scoring essay. The writing step of your essay should take about 15 minutes. That's plenty of time to write three to five solid paragraphs if you work from a prepared outline.

To write your strongest essay, *follow your outline*. You spent five minutes thinking about and organizing your essay, so stick to it. Don't freak out and write from the opposing point-of-view. Trust your outline and yourself.

Remember to write clearly, write concisely, write complete sentences, and use proper grammar. But you only have a few minutes, so write quickly, too. Here is a quickly written essay from our outline.

> The writer hopes that there are enough people in the world who think about others before they think about themselves. While I'm not sure actual "paradise" can be attained, I do think human nature is good enough for us to at least get closer to it. I only have to look as far as my sister for an example of a kind and generous person. But I can also easily cite a celebrity singer, as well as the Congress and the people of the United States, to illustrate the basic goodness of people, and our ability to make the world a better place.
>
> My little sister is 14 years old and a freshman in high school. Some people think that kids this age only think about themselves, their clothes, and MTV. This is not true. My sister is on the soccer team and has a part-time job helping my dad with his cleaning business. She also has her fair share of chores at home. But my little sister still finds time to volunteer every Sunday morning at the soup kitchen at the downtown YMCA. No body told her to do this, she does it because she wants to help others. She is interested in making the world a better place, and she's only 14!
>
> My siste is young, so she can only do so much. But that doesn't mean one person can't make a huge difference on the lives of others. The lead singer of the band

U2, Bono, is an example of this. Bono spends a lot of time when his band isn't touring doing good deeds. In 2002 Bono decided he was going to help the peopl in Africa get wate they could drink. Africa is in a drought and all of the wells have dried up. Bono knows they need to dig deeper wells, but its expensive to do that and they don't have any money. So Bono convinced then U.S. Secretary of the Treasury Paul O'Neil to come to Africa with him. O'Neil did, he saw how much they needed wells, and he came back and told the president.

Once the president was involved, Congress passed a spend bill that will gives over $100 million to Africa to dig these deep wells. These wells are not only going to make life better for Africans, it is going to save lives. But this $100 million doesn't just come out of thin air. Our tax dollars pays for this. That means we, as Americans, are spending money to help people we don't even know. Sure bono makes a big difference, and our elected officials have to get involved, but when it comes right down to it, we are the ones doing the good deed.

In conclusion, I think it is obvious from these examples that people are basic kind and generous. My sister, Bono, former Treasury Secretary O'Neil, and the American people are all examples of people who are putting the happiness of others before their own. We may not get to paradise in a few years, as the author says we might, but we will definitely live in a kinder, friendlier, and safer world.

## Minutes 23–25: Fix

This step takes two minutes. It involves proofreading and fixing your essay. All you'll need to do is fix minor grammatical and/or spelling errors, change a few words here and there, and, maybe, add a sentence or two for clarity's sake.

If you spend the bulk of the 25 minutes thinking about, outlining, and writing the essay, the repair step should entail nothing more than putting the finishing touches on an already strong essay.

Here is our fixed essay:

    The writer <u>Bertrand Faberge</u> hopes that there are enough people in the world who think about others before they think about themselves. While I'm not sure <u>the "paradise" he mentions</u> can be attained, I do think human nature is good enough for us to at least get closer <u>to paradise</u>. I only have to look as far as my sister for an example of a kind and generous person. But I can also easily cite a celebrity singer, as well as the Congress and the people of the United States, to illustrate the basic goodness of people, and our ability to make the world a better place.

    My little sister is 14 years old and a freshman in high school. Some people think that kids this age only think about themselves, their clothes, and MTV. This is not true. My sister is on the soccer team and has a part-time job helping my dad with his cleaning business. She also has her fair share of chores at home. But my little sister still finds time to volunteer every Sunday morning at the soup kitchen at the downtown YMCA. <u>Nobody</u> told her to do <u>this. She</u> does it because she wants to help others. She is interested in <u>making</u> the world a better place, and she's only 14!

    My <u>sister</u> is young, so she can only do so much. But that doesn't mean one person can't make a huge difference <u>in</u> the lives of others. The lead singer of the band U2, Bono, is an example of this. Bono spends a lot of time when his band isn't touring doing good deeds. In 2002 Bono decided he was going to help the <u>people</u> in Africa get <u>water</u> they could drink. Africa is in a drought and all of the <u>shallow</u> wells have dried up. Bono knows they need to dig deeper wells, but its expensive to do that and they don't have any money. So Bono convinced the US Secretary of the Treasury Paul O'Neil to come to Africa with him. O'Neil did, he saw how much they needed wells, and he came back and told the president.

Once the president was involved, Congress passed a <u>spending</u> bill that <u>will give</u> over $100 million to Africa to dig these deep wells. These wells are not only going to <u>improve the lives of</u> Africans, <u>they will also</u> save lives. But this $100 million doesn't just come out of thin air. Our tax dollars pays for this. That means we, as Americans, are spending money to help people we don't even know. <u>Sure, Bono</u> makes a big difference, and our elected officials have to get involved, but when it comes right down to it, we are the ones doing the good deed.

In conclusion, I think it is obvious from these examples that people are <u>basically</u> kind and generous. My sister, Bono, former Treasury Secretary O'Neil, and the American people are all examples of people who are putting the happiness of others before their own. We may not get to paradise in a few years, as the author <u>hopes</u>, but we will definitely live in a kinder, friendlier, and safer world.

Okay, now its your turn. Let's go through each of the steps.

## THINKING PRACTICE

We're going to give you three sample prompts. Look at your watch. Spend exactly two minutes thinking about how you are going to write and deciding whether to agree or disagree with each of these three prompts. Don't write! Think.

### Essay Prompt 1: 2 minutes

"There is nothing like returning to a place that remains unchanged to find the ways in which you yourself have altered."

—Nelson Mandela

**Assignment:** Can going back to a place show you how you have changed? In an essay, support your position by discussing an example (or examples) from literature, science and technology, the arts, current events, or your own experience or observation.

**Essay Prompt 2: 2 minutes**

"People only see what they are prepared to see."

—Ralph Waldo Emerson

**Assignment:** Is what we see and understand affected by what we are ready or want to see? In an essay, support your position by discussing an example (or examples) from literature, science and technology, the arts, current events, or your own experience or observation.

**Essay Prompt 3: 2 minutes**

"If the facts don't fit the theory, change the facts."

—Albert Einstein

"Facts do not cease to exist because they are ignored."

—Aldous Huxley

**Assignment:** Should facts sometimes be ignored? Plan and write an essay in which you develop your point of view on this issue. Support your position with reasoning and examples taken from your reading, studies, experience, or observations.

## ORGANIZING PRACTICE

Read the essay directions below and outline an essay on the topic prompt. Your outline should include the argument you're making, the evidence that supports your argument, and how this information will be arranged in 3–5 paragraphs.

**Directions:** Consider carefully the following statement(s) and the assignment below it.

"It is possible to store the mind with a million facts and still be entirely uneducated."

—Alec Bourne

**Assignment:** Do you think the learning of facts and the development of deeper knowledge are linked, or not? In an essay, support your position by discussing an example (or examples) from literature, science and technology, the arts, current events, or your own experience or observation.

Use this page to outline your essay. We have organized this "scratch paper" a bit for you. On the SAT, you'll have to make do with the margins in your test booklet—that's it. Remember, though, that your essay MUST be written on the lined pages of your answer sheet.

OUTLINE

¶1 (Introduction)
General Argument:

_____

_____

Examples:

_____

¶2: Example 1

_____

_____

_____

¶3: Example 2

_____

_____

_____

¶4: Example 3

_____

_____

_____

¶5 (Conclusion)
Restate general argument in different words

_____

_____

Quickly recap your examples and evidence

_____

_____

## WRITING PRACTICE

Now that you're done with your outline, you're ready to start writing. Here's the prompt again:

**Directions:** Consider carefully the following statement(s) and the assignment below it.

"It is possible to store the mind with a million facts and still be entirely uneducated."

—Alec Bourne

**Assignment:** Do you think the learning of facts and the development of deeper knowledge are linked, or not? In an essay, support your position by discussing an example (or examples) from literature, science and technology, the arts, current events, or your own experience or observation.

Write your draft here.

_____

_____

_____

_____

_____

_____

_____

_____

_____

_____

_____

_____

_____

_____

_____

_____

_____

_____

_____

_____

_____

_____

## FIXING PRACTICE

When you are done, take two minutes to fix spelling, grammar, and any other glaring errors.

## HOW YOUR ESSAY IS GRADED

Unfortunately, we can't send a teacher to your house to grade your paper. But by asking and answering these questions yourself, you'll get a sense of how well you've done.

- Is your essay's argument clear and straightforward?
- Does it address the topic given?
- Does your essay use supporting evidence effectively?
- Is your essay well written?
- Is your essay 4–5 paragraphs long?

## PRACTICE SAT ESSAY

So we took you through TOWF step-by-step. Now you're on your own. Give yourself 25 minutes to put TOWF to work on your own. Again, TOWF stands for:

**T** HINK about the topic (2 minutes)

**O** RGANIZE the paragraphs (5 minutes)

**W** RITE your essay (15 minutes)

**F** IX any mistakes (3 minutes)

After you finish, read the three sample essays—a strong essay, a mediocre essay, and a weak essay—and the sample grader comments. Use these essays and comments to judge the quality of your own essays. Ready? Set your watch and begin.

**Directions:** Consider carefully the following statement(s) and the assignment below it.

> "Whoever controls the media—the images—controls the culture."
>
> —Allen Ginsberg

**Assignment:** Do images presented by the media control culture? In an essay, support your position by discussing an example (or examples) from literature, science and technology, the arts, current events, or your own experience or observation.

Write your outline here.

_____

_____

_____

_____

_____

_____

_____

_____

_____

_____

_____

_____

_____

_____

_____

_____

_____

_____

_____

_____

_____

_____

_____

_____
_____
_____
_____
_____
_____
_____
_____
_____
_____
_____
_____
_____
_____
_____
_____
_____
_____
_____
_____
_____
_____
_____
_____

# SAMPLE OUTLINE

¶1 (Introduction)

General Argument:

Broadcast and print media control many aspects of our culture.

Examples:

Politics and fashion.

¶2: Example 1

Politics—President Bush landed in a fighter jet on an aircraft carrier wearing a combat pilot's flight suit. The image showed Bush as capable commander, patriotic, and "at one" with the armed forces.

¶3: Example 2

Fashion—The ideal female body has changed over the years, depending on the media's ideal. In the 50s, it was Marilyn Monroe's hourglass figure. (Today she would be seen as overweight). In the 90s it was stick-thin "heroin chic" / Kate Moss. Women in the 50s all wanted to be unnaturally busty like Marilyn, because the media told them too. And the women in the 90s wanted to be unnaturally skinny, for the same reason.

¶4 (Conclusion)

Restate general argument in different words

Media is everywhere, and you can't get away from the fact that it controls the way we think and behave.

Quickly recap your examples and evidence

You may not want to believe that being inundated with one type of female body affects you. You may not want to believe that a president's dashing appearance on an aircraft carrier affects your perception of him. But they do.

Write your essay here.

_____
_____
_____
_____
_____
_____
_____
_____
_____
_____
_____
_____
_____
_____
_____
_____
_____
_____
_____
_____
_____
_____

## SAMPLE ESSAYS AND GRADERS' COMMENTS

Three essays follow: a perfect essay, a so-so essay, and a pretty bad essay. Read each and the grader's comments that follow. Which essay does yours most resemble? Do you understand the grader's comments as to why each essay works or doesn't work? What score do you think your essay would get?

### Grade 6 Essay

In today's world, a glut of media images constantly bombards us from all sources—film, television, magazines, newspapers, and the Internet. As a result of this excessive visual stimulation, the media shapes and tailors many of our cultural values to such an extent that we can claim that the media does, indeed, control our culture. Examples of this control can be seen in two distinct and extremely different arenas—politics and fashion.

Contemporary politicians must be prepared to look good and speak articulately on a wide range of issues at all times, especially during a press conference or interview. The images that are captured by the press and transmitted to the public can have a huge impact on a politician's popularity or lack thereof. A prime example of this type of "photo opportunity" came when President Bush, decked out in a full flight-suit, landed on the middle of an aircraft carrier. The image of him in uniform addressing the troops was splashed across the front pages of newspapers everywhere, making the President look not only militarily capable but also patriotic and sympathetic to the men and women serving in the armed forces. By portraying the President in this manner, the media created an impressive and striking image that impacted on the way our culture perceives our leader.

Likewise, fashion magazines present images of female models who are held up as ideals of beauty. In the '50s, photographs of "pin-up girls" with hour-glass figures, like Marilyn Monroe, were prevalent in both magazines and films. As a result, other women strived to imitate the curves and style of these models, who would today be considered overweight. In contrast, the '90s ushered in a new standard of female beauty—the stick-thin and boyish look as epitomized by models like Kate Moss. This "heroin-addict chic" drastically changed the way our culture imagined female beauty, so that actresses like Calista Flockhart or Lara Flynn Boyle became admired for appearing (or being?) anorexic. Clearly, this extreme shift in the cultural ideal for female body types was a direct result of images presented by the media.

Although many people would like to believe that they are not controlled by the female "ideal" being promoted by mainstream media, or by a President's commanding appearance in time of war, the truth is that we are inevitably influenced by our environment and by the images that surround us. Since the media is so prevalent in our daily lives, whether it be television, print, or electronic, we cannot help but be affected by the images our brains receive constantly throughout the day. In this way, then, the claim that images presented by the media can control culture is undoubtedly valid.

**Grader's Comments:** The author begins this essay with a definition of visual media sources and clearly states his opinion of the prompt. The entire essay sticks to the declared topic, with two examples announced at the end of the introduction and developed in detail in the second and third paragraphs.

The essay is well structured, thanks to the use of keywords or phrases (*A prime example, Likewise, As a result, Clearly*) that link the author's ideas together as the essay unfolds. The strong organization of this essay demonstrates that the author took time to plan and outline before writing. In addition, the use of sophisticated language and sentence structure further strengthens this essay and suggests that the author did take time to proofread.

## Grade 4 Essay

The media is a powerful force in American society. More people watch news on TV than read the papers so more people are affected by images presented by the media than by articles written by the media. I don't think these images actively control what our culture is but they certainly have an affect.

For example sports. Athletes are shown playing hard and celebrating hard afterward too. When we see these men and women running down the field or swinging a racket or hitting a ball, we admire what they do and wish we could be like them. Since we admire them we value them and think their worth a lot of money. This makes it acceptable for sports stars to earn huge salaries and get huge bonuses and makes us excuse their unpleasant actions even if they commit crimes or hurt others or cheat or lie. The images we see in the media of these sports heroes definitely make them more acceptable and change the way our culture thinks of these people.

Another example is musicians. Media coverage of concerts or tours can attract fans and sell tickets and souveneers that come from an idea we have of what we'll see when we watch a singer or group perform. But the media can also quickly decide that a certain performer is no longer worthy or important. Look at Michael Jackson. He's definitely displayed some weird behaviors in the passed but the media didn't start to really make him look bad until he was accused of child abuse. Up to that point the press and the images we saw of him made him look odd and unusual but this only helped to make people more interested in him. His actions were always a bit strange and we might have looked down on a "normal" person for doing the same things but since he's a celebrity the media helped to keep his image a certain way so his reputation didn't change.

So media images don't really control our thoughts or actions because we can still think for ourselves. But they do effect us and make us look at things differently. They can also make us change our ideas or beliefs if the images change.

**Grader's Comments:** The author begins her essay with a strong introduction, showing that she understands the prompt. Her perspective on the topic is clearly expressed at the end of the first paragraph and is then supported by two examples, which are fairly well developed.

The organization of the essay is coherent but could be improved by the addition of transitions between paragraphs. The author should be sure to create a plan before she writes in order to make sure that her ideas will flow neatly as she composes her essay.

The weakest parts of this essay are the spelling and grammar errors that occur too frequently. *Souvenirs* (in paragraph 3) is a word frequently used in conversation, but many people can't spell it. There is confusion between *effect* (noun) and *affect* (verb) in paragraph 1; *their* misused for *they're* in the second paragraph; *passed* instead of *past* in the third paragraph. There are sentences fragments in the second, third, and fourth paragraphs; and run-on sentences in the first three paragraphs. This author needs to write more carefully, avoid using too many words she's unsure of, and spend time proofreading so that she can correct these errors.

## Grade 2 Essay

Its silly to think the media can control culture. Sure we see lots of pictures and images if we read newspapers or look at magazines or watch TV or go to movies. But we are not just mindless robots that can't think for themselves. I don't even like all the things I see on TV or in magazines or in movies. And radio is media to but it doesn't have images. Its just sound.

Besides think of all the other things we see that doesn't come from the media. Like other people or buildings or animals or things in nature. These make up our culture two but aren't controlled by some evil media empire.

*And what about poor countries that don't have TV? They still have a culture of some kind so where does it come from if they don't have media images to control it?*

*Saying that media images control our culture is just not true.*

**Grader's Comments:** This essay begins with a simplistic but accurate statement of the author's opinion of the topic in the prompt. However, the author offers little coherent support for his opinion, providing instead several unconnected examples, none of which are well developed. The author needs to spend more time planning his essay before writing.

The essay itself is difficult to follow because it lacks structure and organization. There are no transitions between paragraphs or within each paragraph. For example, the first paragraph jumps from a comparison to robots to a personal opinion to an example of a non-visual type of media. The essay's organization is so poor that the author's meaning is obscured. Spending more time drafting an outline and including transitions and keywords while writing would greatly improve this author's essay.

Finally, there are too many grammatical and spelling errors: *its* misused for *it's* twice in the first paragraph; numerous sentence fragments in the first, second, and third paragraphs; *to* instead of *too* in the first and second paragraphs; *doesn't* instead of *don't* in the second paragraph; and several run-on sentences throughout the essay. This author needs to spend time studying grammar and should leave additional time for proofreading in order to notice and correct some of these errors.

## REMEMBER...

The SAT Essay is graded on a number of different factors, including:

- Length (3–5 paragraphs; each paragraph 2–5 sentences)
- Content (address the topic; write to persuade)
- Neatness (if they can't read it, you'll get a low score)

Kaplan has an attack strategy for writing a high-scoring essay called TOWF:

**T** HINK about the topic (2 minutes)

**O** RGANIZE your paragraphs (5 minutes)

**W** RITE your essay (15 minutes)

**F** IX any mistakes (3 minutes)

You can "self-grade" your essay by asking yourself the following questions about it:

- Is your essay's argument as clear and straightforward?
- Does it address the topic given?
- Does your essay use supporting evidence as effectively?
- Is your essay as well written?
- Is your essay 4–5 paragraphs long?

# Chapter Four: Multiple-Choice Strategies for the New Writing Section

- **Spot the Mistake**
- **Fix the Mistake**
- **Predict the Correction**

As we said in chapter 3, there are two parts to the Writing section: 1) the essay and 2) the multiple-choice questions. The Writing section's three types of multiple-choice questions are like a mini-SAT all to themselves. But don't worry, we've got them covered right here.

## THE NEW SAT WRITING SECTION: MULTIPLE-CHOICE

Each of the SAT Writing question types is based on your catching mistakes (or not) in sentences and short paragraphs. We'll show you how you can catch them. The three kinds of multiple-choice questions are:

- Usage
- Sentence Correction
- Paragraph Correction

Let's deal with them one at a time.

## QUESTION TYPE 1: USAGE QUESTIONS

Usage questions test your ability to spot mistakes in three main areas of written English:

- Basic grammar
- Sentence structure
- Choice of words

Remember, the Writing section measures your ability to recognize acceptable and unacceptable uses of *written* English. Standard *written* English is a bit more formal than the average person's spoken English. Things that you're used to saying in everyday conversation may well be considered wrong when you write them down.

Standard written English is the kind of English that you find in textbooks, and the kind of English your professors will expect you to use on college papers. So that's why they test it on the SAT.

### Directions

The directions for Usage questions will look pretty much like this:

**Directions:** The following sentences contain problems in grammar, usage, diction (choice of words), and idiom.

Some of the sentences are correct.
No sentences contains more than one error.

You will find that the error, if there is one, is underlined and lettered. Elements of the sentence that are not underlined will not be changed. In choosing answers, follow the requirements of standard written English.

If there is an error, select the <u>one underlined part</u> that must be changed to make the sentence correct and fill in the corresponding oval on your answer sheet.

If there is no error, fill in answer oval (E).

EXAMPLE:

<u>Even though</u> he <u>had to</u> supervise a
    A         B
large staff, his salary <u>was no greater</u>
                     C
than <u>a clerk</u>. <u>No error</u>
     D     E                           [Answer: D]

## Spot the Mistake!

All Usage questions are "spot-the-mistake" type questions. You're given a sentence with four words or phrases underlined. The underlined parts are labeled (A) through (D). One of the underlined pieces may contain a grammar mistake. You're supposed to spot it and fill in the corresponding oval on your grid. If the sentence is mistake-free, the correct answer is (E), No error. Here's another one.

Although the number of firms declaring
   A

bankruptcy keep growing, the mayor claims that the
        B                             C

city is thriving. No error
      D       E

So you need to decide which if any underlined word or phrase needs to be changed to make the sentence grammatically correct. You should assume that the parts of the sentence that are not underlined are correct, since they can't be changed.

Here's our four-step strategy for answering Usage questions.

## KAPLAN'S "SPOT-THE-MISTAKE" ATTACK STRATEGY

**Step 1.** Read the whole sentence, "listening" for the mistake.

**Step 2.** If you "heard" the mistake, choose it and you're done.

**Step 3.** If not, read each underlined choice, and eliminate choices that contain no errors.

**Step 4.** Choose the remaining choice (Don't be afraid to choose "E".)

Try this out on our example. Start by reading it to yourself.

Although the number of firms declaring
   A

bankruptcy keep growing, the mayor claims that the
        B                             C

city is thriving. No error
      D     E

Did you hear the mistake? If you did, your work is done; fill in the appropriate oval and move on. If you didn't hear the mistake on the first reading, go back, read each underlined part, and start eliminating underlined parts that are right.

The word *although* seems fine in this context. The word *keep* is a plural verb, but its subject is *number*, which is singular. That seems to be a mistake. The phrase *claims that* sounds all right—it has a singular verb for a singular subject, mayor. Similarly, *is thriving* sounds all right, and it too provides a singular verb for the singular subject city. Choice (B) contains the mistake, so (B) is the correct answer.

Keep in mind that not all the Usage questions on the Writing section contain errors. When you're reading each sentence just to spot mistakes, you may fall into the trap of spotting mistakes where there are none. Choice (E), No error, is the correct answer to Usage questions about one in five times. If you only choose (E) once or twice on the test, chances are that you have spotted mistakes that aren't there.

Try a few practice questions to get the hang of it.

### Spot-the-Mistake Practice

For each of the following questions, choose the best answer from the given choices. Check your answers on page 78.

**Directions:** The following sentences test your knowledge of grammar, usage, diction (choice of words), and idiom.

Some sentences are correct.
No sentence contains more than one error.

You will find that the error, if there is one, is underlined and lettered. Elements of the sentence that are not underlined will not be changed. In choosing answers, follow the requirements of standard written English.

If there is an error, select the <u>one underlined</u> part that must be changed to make the sentence correct and fill in the corresponding oval on your answer sheet.

If there is no error, fill in answer oval (E).

1. Since the government <u>was</u> bankrupt, many of
                               A
   the soldiers <u>which</u> were sent <u>to quell</u> the riots
                      B                   C
   had <u>not been</u> paid in months. <u>No error</u>
              D                              E

2. Although <u>they had been</u> political rivals on
                       A
   <u>more than one</u> occasion, John Quincy Adams
          B
   <u>remained</u> one of Thomas Jefferson's closest
         C
   friends until <u>his</u> death. <u>No error</u>
                      D              E

3. Even <u>those who</u> profess <u>to care</u> about "green"
                A                    B
   issues often fail to consider <u>how</u> their daily
                                      C
   choices <u>effect</u> the environment. <u>No error</u>
               D                              E

4. Ants, <u>which</u> have inhabited the earth for at
               A
   least 100 million years, <u>are without doubt</u> the
                                      B
   <u>more successful</u> of all the social insects of the
         C
   Hymenoptera, an order <u>that also</u> includes
                                  D
   wasps and bees. <u>No error</u>
                         E

5. For my sister and <u>I</u>, the trip to Paris was the
                      A
   <u>fulfillment</u> of a lifelong wish we <u>had scarcely</u>
       B                                        C
   <u>dared to express</u>. <u>No error</u>
         D                    E

6. The volunteers, <u>upon discovering</u> that
                         A
   <u>a large number</u> of the village children <u>were</u>
         B                                        C
   infected by parasites <u>from</u> unclean drinking
                              D
   water, decided to make the well-digging

   project their highest priority. <u>No error</u>
                                       E

7. Although farmers complained that the

   company's new product was expensive,

   malodorous, and <u>dangerous to handle</u>,
                         A
   <u>there was</u> few who <u>would dispute</u> its
       B                      C
   effectiveness <u>as</u> an insecticide. <u>No error</u>
                     D                        E

## QUESTION TYPE 2: SENTENCE CORRECTION QUESTIONS

While the errors in the Usage questions consist of single words or short phrases, the errors in the Sentence Correction questions generally involve the structure of the whole sentence. So, they can be a little harder than Usage questions.

That's the bad part. Here's the good part: While Sentence Correction questions are a little more involved than Usage questions, you have fewer to answer.

### Directions

The directions for Sentence Correction questions will look pretty much like the directions that follow. Read them now so that you don't have to waste time trying to figure out what to do with Sentence Correction questions on test day.

**Directions:** The following sentences test correctness and effectiveness of expression. In choosing answers, follow the requirements of standard written English; that is, pay attention to grammar, choice of words, sentence construction, and punctuation.

In each of the following sentences, part of the sentence or the entire sentence is underlined. Beneath each sentence you will find five ways of phrasing the underlined part. Choice A repeats the original; the other four are different.

Choose the answer that best expresses the meaning of the original sentence. If you think the original is better than any of the alternatives, choose it; otherwise, choose one of the others. Your choice should produce the most effective sentence, clear and precise, without awkwardness or ambiguity.

10. Wanting to reward her assistant for loyalty, <u>Sheila gave a bonus to him as large as his paycheck.</u>

   (A) Sheila gave a bonus to him as large as his paycheck

   (B) given to him by Sheila was a bonus as large as his paycheck

   (C) he was given a bonus as large as his paycheck by Sheila

   (D) Sheila gave him a bonus as large as his paycheck

   (E) Sheila gave him a paycheck to him as large as his bonus          [Answer: D]

## Fix the Mistake!

Remember our "Spot-the-Mistake" strategy from the Usage section? We've got a similar strategy for Sentence Corrections. We call Sentence Correction questions "Fix-the-Mistake" questions because, in addition to finding the mistake in each sentence, you have to pick the answer choice that best corrects it. Like we said, a little harder.

So, in each of these questions, you're given a sentence, part or all of which is underlined. There are five answer choices: the first one reproduces the underlined part of the sentence exactly, and the other four rephrase the underlined portion in various ways.

Here's another example.

> The Emancipation Edict freed the Russian serfs
> in 1861; that being four years before the
> Thirteenth Amendment abolished slavery in
> the United States.
>
> (A) in 1861; that being four years
> (B) in 1861 and is four years
> (C) in 1861 and this amounts to four years
> (D) in 1861, being four years
> (E) in 1861, four years                     [Answer: E]

You have to pick the best choice to replace the underlined portion of the sentence. The correct answer must produce a sentence that's not only grammatically correct, but also effective: it must be clear, precise, and free of awkward verbiage. (Don't know what awkward verbiage is? Anything that sounds like the phrase "awkward verbiage.")

Here is Kaplan's four-step strategy to answering these questions.

## KAPLAN'S "FIX THE MISTAKE" ATTACK STRATEGY

**Step 1.** Read the sentence *carefully* and "listen" for a mistake.
**Step 2.** Identify the error or errors.
**Step 3.** Predict a correction.
**Step 4.** Check the choices for a match that doesn't introduce a new error.

Let's use the method on the example above.

**Step 1. Read the sentence *carefully* and "listen" for a mistake.**
The stem sentence in the example above just doesn't sound right.

**Step 2. Identify the error or errors.**

The semicolon and phrase *that being* sound like the wrong way of joining the two parts of the sentence.

**Step 3. Predict a correction.**

The semicolon and *that being* seem unnecessary. Joining the two sentence fragments with a simple comma would probably work. Plug in your choice to be sure it sounds best.

**Step 4. Check the choices for a match that doesn't introduce a new error.**

Choice (E) has just a comma. Is that enough? All the answer choices begin with *in 1861* and end with *four years*, so you have to look at what comes in between to see what forms the best link. Scan the choices, and you'll find that *and* is in (B), *and this amounts to* in (C), and *being*, preceded by a comma, in (D) are no better than (A).

Choice (E) is the best way to rewrite the underlined portion of the sentence, so (E) is the correct answer.

Remember, not every sentence contains an error: Choice (A) is correct about one-fifth of the time. In any event, since you should begin by reading the original sentence carefully, you should *never* waste time reading choice (A). Time = points, and this is another great SAT time saver.

Try a few practice questions to get the hang of it.

## Fix-the-Mistake Practice

For each of the following questions, choose the best answer from the given choices. Check your answers on page 79.

**Directions:** The following sentences test correctness and effectiveness of expression. In choosing answers, follow the requirements of standard written English; that is, pay attention to grammar, choice of words, sentence construction, and punctuation.

In each of the following sentences, part of the sentence or the entire sentence is underlined. Beneath each sentence you will find five ways of phrasing the underlined part. Choice A repeats the original; the other four are different.

Choose the answer that best expresses the meaning of the original sentence. If you think the original is better than any of the alternatives, choose it; otherwise, choose one of the others. Your choice should produce the most effective sentence, clear and precise, without awkwardness or ambiguity.

1. Patients with Alzheimer's disease typically exhibit symptoms such as confusion, memory loss, <u>and their language skills are impaired.</u>

   (A) and their language skills are impaired.

   (B) and it also impairs their language skills.

   (C) and impaired language skills.

   (D) besides their language skills being
         impaired.

   (E) in addition to their language skills being
         impaired.

2. <u>Upon entering the jail, the prisoners' personal belongings are surrendered to the guards.</u>

   (A) Upon entering the jail, the prisoners' personal belongings are surrendered to the guards.

   (B) Upon entering the jail, the prisoners surrender their personal belongings to the guards.

   (C) The prisoners' personal belongings having been surrendered to the guards upon entering the jail.

   (D) Upon entering the jail, the guards are to whom the prisoners surrender their personal belongings.

   (E) Upon entering the jail, the prisoners will have been surrendering their personal belongings to the guards.

3. <u>The albatross has a broad wingspan, it is graceful in the air but ungainly on dry land.</u>

   (A) The albatross has a broad wingspan, it is graceful in the air but ungainly on dry land.

   (B) The albatross, with its broad wingspan, is graceful in the air but ungainly on dry land.

   (C) Having a broad wingspan, the albatross is graceful in the air, however it is ungainly on dry land.

   (D) The albatross, which has a broad wingspan, graceful in the air but ungainly on dry land.

   (E) The albatross, although having a broad wingspan, is graceful in the air but ungainly on dry land.

4. King John of England is remembered not so much for his administrative successes <u>but for failing in military engagements</u>.

    (A) but for failing in military engagements

    (B) but more for the fact that he failed in military engagements

    (C) than he was for having failed militarily

    (D) the reason being that he failed in military engagements

    (E) as for his military failures

5. According to older fishermen, cod and haddock were once plentiful in the North Sea, but years of over-fishing and pollution have <u>had a negative overall impact on the fish stocks.</u>

    (A) had a negative overall impact on the fish stocks.

    (B) impacted the fish stocks negatively.

    (C) the result that the fish stocks are diminished.

    (D) depleted the fish stocks.

    (E) been depleting the fish stocks overall.

6. <u>During the winter months, several feet of snow
   cover the narrow mountain pass, which is the
   only route to the monastery.</u>

   (A) During the winter months, several feet of
       snow cover the narrow mountain pass,
       which is the only route to the
       monastery.

   (B) The only route to the monastery, several
       feet of snow cover the narrow mountain
       pass during the winter months.

   (C) Several feet of snow cover the narrow
       mountain pass during the winter
       months which is the only route to the
       monastery.

   (D) Several feet of snow cover the narrow
       mountain pass, which is the only route
       to the monastery during the winter
       months.

   (E) During the winter months, covering the
       narrow mountain pass which is the only
       route to the monastery is snow.

7. The Townshend Acts, a piece of British legislation enacted on June 29, 1767, <u>were intended for the raising of revenue, to tighten customs enforcement, and assert</u> imperial authority in America.

(A) were intended for the raising of revenue, to tighten customs enforcement, and assert

(B) were intended to raise revenue, tighten customs enforcement, and assert

(C) were with the intention of raising revenue, tightening customs enforcement, and assert

(D) had for their intention the raising of revenue, tightening of customs enforcement, and asserting

(E) were intended to raise revenue, also to tighten customs enforcement and assert

## QUESTION TYPE 3: PARAGRAPH CORRECTION QUESTIONS

Paragraph Correction questions follow short essays that are three to five paragraphs long. The short essays can be about any topic. You do not have to know anything about the topic.

Most Paragraph Correction questions ask you to clean up awkward and ambiguous sentences. The most important thing with these questions is their *context*. You can't determine the best way to repair bad sentences without knowing what comes before and after them.

A few Paragraph Correction questions will also ask you about the overall organization of the essay. Again, context is critical. You can't, for example, decide which of five sentences best concludes an essay without knowing what the essay is all about.

## Directions

Here they are. You know the drill.

**Directions:** The passage below is an early draft of an essay. Parts of the passage need to be rewritten.

Read the passage and answer the questions that follow. Some questions are about individual sentences or parts of sentences; in these questions, you are asked to select the choice that will improve sentence structure and word choice. Other questions refer to parts of the essay or the entire essay and ask you to consider the organization and development of the essay. You should follow the conventions of standard written English in answering the questions. After you have chosen your answer, fill in the corresponding oval on your answer sheet.

Whadya know, we've got a strategy for this kind of question, too.

## KAPLAN'S "PREDICT THE CORRECTION" ATTACK STRATEGY

Kaplan's strategy works for all kinds of Paragraph Correction questions.

**Step 1.** Read the passage quickly for the overall idea and tone.

**Step 2.** Read the question.

**Step 3.** Reread the relevant text and consider its context.

**Step 4.** Predict the correction.

**Step 5.** Choose the best match.

### Step 1: Read the passage quickly for the overall idea and tone

Read the entire essay quickly. Get a sense of the essay's main idea, as well as the main idea of each paragraph. This will come in handy when you're asked to answer questions about the essay as a whole.

### Step 2: Read the question

Now read the question closely. Make sure that you understand exactly what you're asked to do. Questions that require you to revise or combine sentences will supply you with the sentence numbers. Questions that ask about the entire essay generally won't refer to specific sentences.

### Step 3: Reread the relevant text and consider its context

Go back and reread that sentence or two that the question is about. But don't stop there. This next part is very important: Also reread the sentences before and after the target sentence(s). Rereading the lines around the target sentence(s) will provide you with its context. Context helps you to choose the best construction from among the answer choices.

*Note:* For those questions about the essay as a whole, skim quickly over the entire essay to familiarize yourself with its contents.

### Step 4: Predict the correction

Say to yourself what you think the correct sentence structure should be.

### Step 5: Choose the best match

Go to the answer choices and pick the choice that best matches the sentence in your head. Make sure the one you pick doesn't introduce a new mistake into the sentence.

So, to summarize: **read** the essay quickly; **read** the question; **reread** the target sentences and the sentences that surround them; **make up** a sentence that would eliminate the mistake; and **choose** the answer choice that best matches your sentence.

Let's see how it works on the three kinds of Paragraph Correction questions, shall we?

## The Three Kinds of Paragraph Correction Questions

There are three basic types of Paragraph Correction questions:

- General organization questions
- Revising sentences questions
- Combining sentences questions

### 1. General Organization Questions

If you've got a firm grasp of the essay after you first read through it, you should jump right to the general organization questions first. Do these questions while the essay is fresh in your mind.

On the other hand, if your grasp of the essay is a bit shaky, work on general organization questions last. Start with questions that ask you to revise or combine sentences. Doing so should improve your grasp of the overall essay, making it easier for you to tackle the general organization questions later.

### 2. Revising Sentences Questions

Take a look at the following paragraph and question. The question focuses on a single word in one sentence, but in order to answer this typical example of a revision question, you'll need to reread the entire paragraph.

(1) *The Spanish-American War was one of the shortest and most decisive wars ever fought.* (2) *The postwar settlement, the Treaty of Paris, reflected the results of the fighting.* (3) *Under its terms, Spain was compelled to cede large territories in North America and the Pacific.* (4) *The United States gained control over some of these territories, including Puerto Rico and Guam.* (5) *It was reduced in status from a major to a minor power.* (6) *The United States, in contrast, emerged from the war as a world power, and would soon go on to become a major participant in Asian and European affairs.*

In context, which is the best version of the underlined part of sentence 5?

*It was reduced* in status from a major to a minor power.

(A)  (As it is now)

(B)  Spain was reduced

(C)  The war caused Spain to be reduced

(D)  As a result of the war, it had been reduced

(E)  It had now been reduced                    [Answer: B]

Sentence 5 refers to Spain's status. That much should have been clear to you by reading sentences 2, 3, 4, and 6. The pronoun *it*, however, makes sentence 5 ambiguous. What does it refer to? To make this sentence less ambiguous, it should be changed to the noun *Spain*. That leaves (B) and (C) as possible correct answers. Since (B) is a more concise and less awkward construction than (C), (B) is correct.

## 3. Combining Sentences

Take a look at the following paragraph and question.

(6) *Albert Einstein was a great physicist.* (7) *He won a Nobel Prize in Physics.* (8) *He got the prize for his research into the photoelectric effect.* (9) *Later physicists demonstrated the validity of Einstein's ideas.*

Which of the following is the best way to combine sentences 7 and 8?

*He won a Nobel Prize in Physics. He got the prize for his research into the photoelectric effect.*

(A)  The Nobel Prize in Physics that he won was for his research into the photoelectric effect.

(B)  Having researched the photoelectric effect, he won a Nobel Prize in Physics.

(C)  He won a Nobel Prize in Physics for his research into the photoelectric effect.

(D)  He got the prize in physics, the Noble Prize in Physics, for his research into the photoelectric effect.

(E)  Because of his research into the photoelectric effect he got the Nobel Prize in Physics.

[Answer: C]

Did you choose (C)? It's the best written and most economical of the choices. Whether you're asked to revise or combine sentences, the correct answer will often (but not always) be the shortest answer. Good writing is concise.

## Predict-the-Correction Practice

Use everything you have learned about combining sentences, revising sentences, and answering "big picture" questions on the following sample essays and questions.

For each of the following questions, choose the best answer from the given choices. Check your answers on page 80.

**Directions:** The passage below is an early draft of an essay. Parts of the passage need to be rewritten.

Read the passage and answer the questions that follow. Some questions are about individual sentences or parts of sentences; in these questions, you are asked to select the choice which will improve sentence structure and word choice. Other questions refer to parts of the essay or the entire essay and ask you to consider the organization and development of the essay. You should follow the conventions of standard written English in answering the questions. After you have chosen your answer, fill in the corresponding oval on your answer sheet.

Questions 1–8 are based on the following essay, which is a response to an assignment to write a letter to a local newspaper protesting cuts in funding for after-school sports programs.

(1) *I disagree with the editor's view that after-school sports programs should be cut in our city government's search for ways to reduce spending.* (2) *The editor argues that extra-curricular sports play a less important role to academic studies, distracting students from the opportunity to increase their knowledge after school is out.* (3) *However, I myself believe that playing sports enhances students' academic performance.* (4) *Why is sports so effective in this regard?* (5) *The main reason is that sports teaches people to excel.* (6) *It gives students the chance to strive for greatness.* (7) *It shows them that it takes courage and discipline to succeed in competition with others.* (8) *Top athletes such as Michael Jordan become role models for young people everywhere, inspiring them with his brilliant individual performances.* (9) *In addition to these personal attributes, playing in team sports show young people how to interact with each other,*

*achieving shared goals. (10) Such principles have a direct impact on how students perform in their academic studies. (11) I know that being selected for the school lacrosse team taught me many valuable lessons about working with others. (12) Not only that, friendships which I have made there were carried into the rest of my school life. (13) In summary, I would urge the editor to strongly reconsider his stance on extra-curricular sports. (14) There are doubtless other ways of city government saving the money they require.*

1. Which of the following is the best way to revise the underlined portion of sentence 3 (reproduced below)?

   *However, I myself believe that playing sports enhances students' academic performance.*

   (A) However, I myself believe that playing sports should enhance

   (B) Playing sports, however, I believe enhances

   (C) However, I personally believe that playing sports enhances

   (D) I believe, however, that playing sports enhances

   (E) However, I myself believe that to play sports is to enhance

2. Which of the following is the best way to revise and combine sentences 6 and 7 (reproduced below)?

*It gives students the chance to strive for greatness. It shows them that it takes courage and discipline to succeed in competition with others.*

(A) Although it gives students the chance to strive for greatness, it also shows them that it takes courage and discipline to succeed in competition with others.

(B) While it gives students the chance to strive for greatness, also showing them that it takes courage and discipline to succeed in competition with others.

(C) It gives students the chance to strive for greatness, showing them that it takes courage and discipline to succeed in competition with others.

(D) Because it gives students the chance to strive for greatness, they are shown that it takes courage and discipline to succeed in competition with others.

(E) It gives students the chance to strive for greatness and show them that it takes courage and discipline to succeed in competition with others.

3. In the context of the second paragraph, which of the following is the best version of the underlined portion of sentence 8 (reproduced below)?

*Top athletes such as Michael Jordan become role models for young people everywhere, inspiring them with his brilliant individual performances.*

(A) (As it is now)

(B) inspiring him with their

(C) inspiring them with their

(D) to inspire them with his

(E) inspiring him with his

4. Which of the following is the best way to revise the underlined portion of sentence 12 (reproduced below)?

*Not only that, friendships which I have made there were carried into the rest of my school life.*

(A) And,

(B) Moreover,

(C) Nevertheless,

(D) Sequentially,

(E) Finally,

5. Which of the following best describes the author's approach in the passage as a whole?

   (A) defending an unpopular point of view

   (B) criticizing an opponent's opinion

   (C) supporting an argument with evidence

   (D) considering the merits of two competing proposals

   (E) citing statistics to disprove a theory

6. The author could best improve sentence 14 (reproduced below) by

   *There are doubtless other ways of city government saving the money they require.*

   (A) making an analogy to historical events

   (B) taking alternative points of view into account

   (C) including a personal anecdote about her participation in team sports

   (D) speculating about the motivations of those advocating cuts

   (E) providing examples of other areas in which spending could be reduced

## Remember...

**Usage** questions test your knowledge of:

- Basic grammar
- Sentence structure
- Word choice

All usage questions are "spot-the-mistake" questions.

Kaplan has a strategy for spotting usage mistakes:

Step 1. Read the whole sentence, "listening" for the mistake.

Step 2. If you "heard" the mistake, choose it and you're done.

Step 3. If not, read each underlined choice, and eliminate choices that contain no errors.

Step 4. Choose the remaining choice (Don't be afraid to choose "E".)

**Sentence Correction** questions test a small number of grammar issues.

With sentence corrections, you have to fix the mistake, not just spot it.

Kaplan has a strategy for fixing sentences:

Step 1. Read the sentence carefully and "listen" for a mistake.

Step 2. Identify the error or errors.

Step 3. Predict a correction.

Step 4. Check the choices for a match that doesn't introduce a new error.

The most important thing about **Paragraph Correction** questions is knowing their *context*. There are three basic types of Paragraph Correction questions:

- General organization sentences
- Revising sentences questions
- Combining sentences questions

Kaplan has a "predict-the-correction" strategy that works for every kind of Paragraph Correction question.

Step 1. Read the passage quickly for the overall idea and tone.

Step 2. Read the question.

Step 3. Reread relevant portion and its context.

Step 4. Predict the correction.

Step 5. Check the choices for a match that doesn't introduce a new error.

## Answers and Explanations

### Usage Questions

**1. B**

The relative pronoun *which* refers to the soldiers, but *which* cannot be used to refer to people, only to things. The sentence should use the word *who* instead.

**2. D**

Another pronoun error: in this sentence, it is not clear whether *his* refer to Adams or to Jefferson; hence this sentence contains a vague pronoun reference.

**3. D**

*Affect* and *effect* are commonly confused words. Here, *affect* (meaning "to influence" or "to have an *effect* on") would be the correct word, not *effect*.

**4. C**

Faulty comparison: ants are being compared to all the other social insects in the *Hymenoptera* order. Since this order includes far more than two insect species, the superlative *most successful* should be used instead of the comparative *more successful*.

**5. A**

Take out the words "my sister and," and the error of pronoun case becomes obvious you wouldn't say "for *I*." Since this pronoun is the object of the preposition *for*, it should be in the objective case: for my sister and *me*.

**6. E**

The sentence contains no error.

**7. B**

In the second half of the sentence, the verb *was* does not agree with its subject, *few*. *Few* is a plural noun, so the sentence should read *there were few*. Be careful when the subject follows the verb.

## Sentence Correction Questions

### 1. C

For the sake of parallelism, all three things in this list must be in the same grammatical form. *Confusion* and *memory loss* are both nouns, so *impaired language skills* is the best choice to complete the sentence.

### 2. B

*Upon entering the jail* is an introductory participial phrase that describes the prisoners (they are the ones entering the jail). As the sentence is worded, it sounds as though the prisoners' personal belongings are entering the jail. (B) and (E) are the only two choices that place *the prisoners* right next to the phrase that describes them. (B) is the best choice; (E) puts the verb in an awkward and incorrect tense.

### 3. B

Choice (B) is the best way to rephrase this run-on sentence; it expresses, in an economical and graceful way, the logical connection between these two pieces of information about the albatross.

### 4. E

*So much* should be followed by the preposition *as*. Choice (E) completes the comparison and conforms to the rules of parallelism; *administrative successes* (an adjective-noun pair) is balanced by *military failures*.

### 5. D

The underlined portion of the sentence is wordy and awkward; it sounds like a badly written business memo. Choice (D) is a concise and correct rephrasing (note that it is also the shortest answer choice).

### 6. A

The sentence contains no error. Choices (B) through (E) are all awkward or grammatically incorrect.

### 7. B

The three items in this list should be in parallel grammatical form. The best way to correct the error is to rephrase all three as infinitive verbs (note, again, that the correct answer is also the shortest and most concise).

## Paragraph Correction Questions

### 1. D

The key to this problem is realizing that *I myself* is redundant. If the author has already used *I*, there's no need to add *myself* to clarify. Choice (D) provides the best fix here; notice that it's also the shortest, most straightforward answer. Choice (A) and (E) still include *myself*. Choice (C) substitutes another redundancy—the word *personally*. Choice (B) is unnecessarily convoluted, and is missing a comma following *I believe*.

### 2. C

The context here suggests a strong link between the two sentences: sports provide students with the chance to strive for greatness *by* showing them it takes courage, etc. Choice (C) is the best answer. Choice (A) introduces an illogical contrast. Choice (B) creates a sentence fragment. Choice (D) uses the passive voice unnecessarily. In (E), the verb *show* doesn't agree with the subject *it*.

### 3. C

The key to this sentence is spotting a subject-verb agreement problem. The subject in the sentence is *top athletes*, not *Michael Jordan*; he is only introduced as an example of a top athlete. So the underlined pronouns should be *them* (to agree with *young people*) and *their* (to agree with *top athletes*).

### 4. B

To fix this ambiguous introductory phrase, you're looking for a conjunction that expresses the idea of listing an *additional benefit* of participation in team sports. Choice (B) *moreover* does this effectively. (A)'s *and* is not an idiomatic conjunction with which to begin a sentence. Choice (C) creates an unnecessary contrast. In (D), *sequentially* means *in order*, not *consequently*. Choice (E), finally, is wrong because this sentence describes the second item in a list of two.

## 5. C

The author states her opinion outright at the end of paragraph 1, backing it up with evidence in paragraph 2, making (C) the best answer. Choice (A) is wrong because there's no suggestion it's an unpopular point of view. Choice (B) is wrong because the author doesn't waste time criticizing the editor's standpoint. Choice (D) is out because no space is devoted to considering the editor's proposal in fact, the passage isn't about a specific proposal at all. Finally, (E) is wrong because no statistics are mentioned.

## 6. E

Sentence 14 provides a weak ending to the passage because it refers to *other ways of the city government saving money* without suggesting what these might be. So the best improvement to sentence 14 might be (E) providing examples of alternative areas for cuts. Choice (A) would be an odd solution—historical events haven't been mentioned thus far in the passage. Choice (B) would weaken the essay just at the point at which the author needs to strengthen it. Choice (C) would be repetitive since the author has already included a personal anecdote. Finally, (D) would simply offer a digression at this point.

# Chapter Five: 10 BASIC SAT MATH CONCEPTS

- Remainders, Averages, Ratios, Rates
- Percents, Combinations, Simultaneous Equations
- Symbols, Special Triangles, Multiple and Strange Figures

The SAT Math section has always tested certain topics of basic math. When you are confident that you understand these basic math concepts, the SAT Math section gets a whole lot easier. This chapter introduces you to these basic math concepts and explains how the SAT tests them. We also teach you our techniques for solving these problems and how these techniques will work with both types of SAT Math questions: regular math and Grid-ins.

## BASIC MATH
These are the 10 basic math concepts the SAT tests:
1. Remainders
2. Averages
3. Ratios
4. Rates
5. Percents
6. Combinations
7. Simultaneous equations
8. Symbols
9. Special triangles
10. Multiple and strange figures

## Remainders

Remainder questions can be easier than they seem. Many students believe that the key to solving a remainder question is to find the value of a variable, which takes up a lot of time and causes confusion. However, that type of problem solving is usually not necessary. For example, look at the following remainder problem.

> When $n$ is divided by 7, the remainder is 4.
> What is the remainder when $2n$ is divided
> by 7?
>
> (A) 0
>
> (B) 1
>
> (C) 2
>
> (D) 3
>
> (E) 4                [Answer: B]

This question doesn't depend on knowing the value of $n$. In fact, $n$ has an infinite number of possible values. The easy way to solve this kind of problem is to pick a number for $n$. Because the remainder when $n$ is divided by 7 is 4, pick any multiple of 7 and add 4. The easiest multiple to work with is 7. So, $7 + 4 = 11$. Plug 11 in for $n$ and see what happens:

What is the remainder when $2n$ is divided by 7?

What is the remainder when $2(11)$ is divided by 7?

What is the remainder when 22 is divided by 7?

$\dfrac{22}{7} = 3$ remainder 1

The remainder is 1 when $n = 11$. So the answer is (B). The remainder will also be 1 when $n = 18, 25,$ or 46.

## Averages

Instead of giving you a list of values to plug into the average formula $\dfrac{\text{Sum of Terms}}{\text{Number of Terms}}$, SAT average questions often put a spin on the problem, like so:

The average weight of five amplifiers in a guitar shop is 32 pounds. If four of the amplifiers weigh 25, 27, 19, and 35 pounds, what is the weight of the fifth amplifier?

(A) 28 pounds

(B) 32 pounds

(C) 49 pounds

(D) 54 pounds

(E) 69 pounds                    [Answer: D]

This problem tells you the average of a group of terms and asks you to find the value of a missing term. To get the answer, you need to work with the sum. Let the variable $x$ = the weight of the fifth amplifier. Plug this into the average formula:

$$\text{Average} = \frac{\text{Sum of Terms}}{\text{Number of Terms}}$$

$$32 = \frac{25 + 27 + 19 + 35 + x}{5}$$

$$32 \times 5 = 25 + 27 + 19 + 35 + x$$

The average weight of the amplifiers times the number of amplifiers equals the total weight of the amplifiers. The new formula is

Average × Number of Terms = Sum of Terms.

Remember this version of the average formula so you can find the total sum whenever you know the average of a group of terms and the number of terms. Now you can solve for the weight of the fifth amplifier as follows:

$$32 \times 5 = 25 + 27 + 19 + 35 + x$$

$$160 = 106 + x$$

$$54 = x$$

So, the weight of the fifth amplifier is 54 pounds, choice (D).

## Ratios

SAT test makers often write ratio questions in a way that tricks you into setting up the wrong ratio. Don't be angry with them. Understand that they can't help themselves, and calmly work around their tricks.

Try to work through the question below.

> Out of every 50 CDs produced in a certain
> factory, 20 are scratched. What is the ratio of
> unscratched CDs produced to scratched CDs
> produced?
>
> (A) 2:5
> (B) 3:5
> (C) 2:3
> (D) 3:2
> (E) 5:2                                    [Answer: D]

You need to find the parts and the whole in this problem. In this
case, the total number of CDs is the whole, and the numbers of
unscratched CDs and scratched CDs, respectively, are the parts that
make up this whole. You're given a part-to-whole ratio (the ratio of
scratched CDs to all CDs) and asked to find a part-to-part ratio (the
ratio of unscratched CDs to scratched CDs).

If 20 CDs of every 50 are scratched, the remaining 30 CDs must be
OK. So, the part-to-part ratio of good-to-scratched CDs is 30:20, or
3:2, choice (D). If you hadn't identified the part and the whole first, it
would have been easy to become confused and compared a part to
the whole, like the ratios in answer choices (A), (B), and (E).

This approach also works for ratio questions where you need to find
actual quantities. Here's an example.

Of every 5 CDs produced in a certain factory, 2 are scratched. If
2,200 CDs were produced, how many were scratched?

Here you need to find a quantity: the number of defective CDs. If
you're looking for the actual quantities in a ratio, set up and solve a
proportion. You're given a part-to-whole ratio (the ratio of scratched
CDs to all CDs) and the total number of CDs produced. You can find
the answer by setting up and solving a proportion:

$$\frac{\text{Number of Scratched CDs}}{\text{Total Number of CDs}} = \frac{2}{5} = \frac{x}{2{,}200}$$

$x$ = number of scratched CDs

$5x = 4{,}400$ (by cross-multiplying $\frac{2}{5} = \frac{x}{2{,}200}$)

$x = 880$ (by dividing both sides by 5)

Remember that ratios compare only relative size; they don't tell you the actual quantities involved. Distinguish clearly between the parts and the whole in ratio problems.

## Rates

A rate is a ratio that compares quantities represented by different units. In the following problem, the units are dollars and the number of headphones.

> If 8 headphones cost $a$ dollars, $b$ headphones would cost how many dollars?

(A) $8ab$

(B) $\dfrac{8a}{b}$

(C) $\dfrac{8}{ab}$

(D) $\dfrac{a}{8b}$

(E) $\dfrac{ab}{8}$ [Answer: E]

This rate problem at first seems difficult because of the variables. It's hard to get a clear picture of what the relationship is between the units. You need to pick numbers for the variables to find the context of that relationship.

Pick numbers for $a$ and $b$ that will be easy for you to work with in the problem. Let $a = 16$. Then, 8 headphones will cost $16. So the cost per headphone at this rate $\dfrac{\$16}{8 \text{ headphones}} = \$2$ per headphone. Let $b = 5$. Therefore, the cost of 5 headphones at this rate will be 5 headphones $\times$ \$2 per headphone $= \$10$.

Now plug $a = 16$ and $b = 5$ into the answer choices to see which one gives you a value of 10.

(A) $8 \times 16 \times 5 = 640$. Eliminate.

(B) $\dfrac{8 \times 16}{5} = \dfrac{128}{5}$. Eliminate.

(C) $\dfrac{8}{16 \times 5} = \dfrac{1}{10}$. Eliminate.

(D) $\dfrac{16}{8 \times 5} = \dfrac{2}{5}$. Eliminate.

(E) $\dfrac{16 \times 5}{8} = 10$

Because (E) is the only one that gives the correct value, it is the correct answer.

## Percents

In percent problems, you're usually given two pieces of information and asked to solve for a third value, as in the following question.

> Last year Aunt Edna's annual salary was $20,000. This year's raise brings her to an annual salary of $25,000. If she gets a raise of the same percentage every year, what will her salary be next year?
>
> (A) $27,500
> (B) $30,000
> (C) $31,250
> (D) $32,500
> (E) $35,000                    [Answer: C]

When you see a percent problem, remember the following formulas:

If you are solving for a percent: $\dfrac{\text{Part}}{\text{Whole}} = \text{Percent}$

If you need to solve for a part: Percent × Whole = Part

This problem asks for Aunt Edna's projected salary for next year—that is, her current salary plus her next raise. You know last year's salary ($20,000), and you know this year's salary ($25,000), so you can find the difference between the two salaries: $25,000 − $20,000 = $5,000 = her raise.

Now, your next step is to find the percent this raise represents by using the formula Percent = $\dfrac{\text{Part}}{\text{Whole}}$. Because Aunt Edna's raise was calculated on last year's salary, divide by $20,000. Be sure you know which *whole* to plug in. Here, you're looking for a percentage of $20,000, not of $25,000.

Percent = $\dfrac{\$5,000}{\$20,000} = \dfrac{1}{4} =$ , or 25%

You know Aunt Edna will get the same percent raise next year, so solve for the part. Use the formula Percent × Whole = Part. Make sure you change the percent to either a fraction or a decimal before beginning calculations.

Her raise next year will be 25% × $25,000 = $\dfrac{1}{4}$ × 25,000 = $6,250.

Add that amount to this year's salary and you have her projected salary: $25,000 + $6,250 = $31,250, or answer (C).

Aunt Edna must be doing something right.

## Combinations

Combination problems ask you to find the different possibilities that can occur in a given situation. The order of events is not important.

If Alice, Betty, and Carlos sit in three adjacent empty seats in a movie house, how many different seating arrangements are possible?

(A) 3
(B) 4
(C) 5
(D) 6
(E) 8                    [Answer: D]

To solve this question, you need to find the number of possibilities by listing them in a quick but systematic way. Let the first letter of each name stand for that person. First, find all the combinations with Alice in the first seat as follows:

ABC

ACB

Use the same system, putting Betty in the first seat, and then Carlos. You get the combinations:

BAC

BCA

CAB

CBA

At this point, we've exhausted every possibility. There are six possible arrangements, so (D) is the correct answer. Some problems set up conditions that limit the possibilities somewhat. Some may ask for the number of distinct possibilities, meaning that if the same combination shows up twice in different forms, you should count it only once. Consider the following problem.

Set I: {2, 3, 4, 5}
Set II: {1, 2, 3}
If *x* is a number generated by multiplying a
number from Set I by a number from Set II,
how many possible values of *x* are greater
than 5?

(A) 3

(B) 4

(C) 5

(D) 6

(E) 7                                    [Answer: D]

Again, list the possibilities in a systematic way, pairing off each number in the first set with each number in the second set, so every combination is included. The following list is a good example of how this strategy works.

| | |
|---|---|
| $2 \times 1 = 2$ | $4 \times 1 = 4$ |
| $2 \times 2 = 4$ | $4 \times 2 = 8$ |
| $2 \times 3 = 6$ | $4 \times 3 = 12$ |
| $3 \times 1 = 3$ | $5 \times 1 = 5$ |
| $3 \times 2 = 6$ | $5 \times 2 = 10$ |
| $3 \times 3 = 9$ | $5 \times 3 = 15$ |

Always write down the possibilities as you organize them, so you can count them accurately, and so you don't count the same combination twice. How many of these values are greater than 5? Going down the list: 6, 6, 9, 8, 12, 10, and 15. Although there are 7 answers for *x* that are greater than 5, two of them are the same. There are six different values of *x* greater than 5, not 7. The answer is (D). Here, it would have been very easy to quickly take seven as the correct answer and miss the last step. Be sure you carefully consider every possibility and loose end before moving on. We will teach you how to recognize and avoid traps like this one in chapter 7.

## Simultaneous Equations

To get a numerical value for each variable in a simultaneous equation, you need as many different equations as there are variables. So, if you have two variables, you need two distinct equations. Let's look at the following example.

$$\text{If } p + 2q = 14 \text{ and } 3p + q = 12, \text{ then } p =$$

*Note:* This is a Grid-in, so you'll have to come up with the correct answer on our own.

You could tackle this problem by solving for one variable in terms of the other and then plugging this expression into the other equation. But the simultaneous equations that appear on the SAT can usually be handled in an easier way. Combine the equations, by adding or subtracting them, to cancel out all but one of the variables. You can't eliminate $p$ or $q$ by adding or subtracting the equations in their present forms. But, if you multiply the second equation by 2, you'll have this equation:

$$2(3p + q) = 2(12)$$
$$6p + 2q = 24$$

With this new equation, subtracting one equation from the other is easier because the $q$s will cancel out, so you can solve for $p$:

$$\begin{array}{r} 6p + 2q = 24 \\ -[p + 2q = 14] \\ \hline 5p + 0 = 10 \end{array}$$

If $5p = 10$, $p = 2$. On the answer sheet, you would grid in the answer 2.

## Symbols

You should be quite familiar with the arithmetic symbols $+$, $-$, $\times$, $\div$. Finding the value of $10 + 2$, $18 - 4$, $4 \times 9$, or $96 \div 16$ is easy. However, on the SAT, you may come across bizarre symbols. You may even be asked to find the value of $10 \star 2$, $5 \circledast 7$, $10 \circledast 6$, or $65 \heartsuit 2$.

The SAT puts strange symbols in questions to confuse or unnerve you. Don't let them succeed. The question stem always tells you what the strange symbol means. Although this type of question may look difficult, it is really an exercise in plugging in numbers. Look at the following example:

If $a \star b = \sqrt{a+b}$ for all non-negative numbers, what is the value of $10 \star 6$?

(A) 0

(B) 2

(C) 4

(D) 8

(E) 16                    [Answer: C]

To solve, just plug in 10 for $a$ and 6 for $b$ into the expression $\sqrt{a+b}$. That equals $\sqrt{10+6}$, or $\sqrt{16} = 4$, choice (C). Don't freak out; plug in the numbers, and you'll be fine.

## Special Triangles

Look for the special triangles in geometry problems. Special triangles contain a lot of information. For instance, if you know the length of one side of a 30-60-90 triangle, you can easily work out the lengths of the others. Special triangles allow you to transfer one piece of information around the whole figure.

The following are the special triangles you should look for on the SAT. You don't have to memorize the ratios (they're listed in the instructions), but you should be able to recognize them when you see them.

### Equilateral Triangles

All interior angles are 60 degrees, and all sides have equal length.

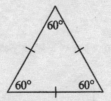

## Isosceles Triangles

Two sides have equal length, and the angles facing these sides are equal.

## Right Triangles

These contain a 90-degree angle. The sides are related by the Pythagorean theorem: $a^2 + b^2 = c^2$, where $a$ and $b$ are the legs and $c$ is the hypotenuse.

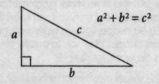

$$a^2 + b^2 = c^2$$

## The "Special" Right Triangles

Many triangle problems contain *special* right triangles in which the side lengths always come in predefined ratios. If you recognize them, you won't have to use the Pythagorean theorem to find the value of a missing side length.

## The 3-4-5 Right Triangle

(Be on the lookout for multiples of 3-4-5 as well.)

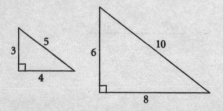

## The Isosceles Right Triangle

(Note the side ratio: 1 to 1 to $\sqrt{2}$.)

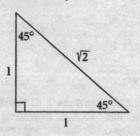

## The 30-60-90 Right Triangle

(Note the side ratio: 1 to $\sqrt{3}$ to 2, and note which side is opposite which angle.)

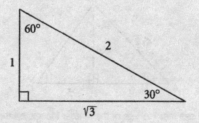

Now that we've gone through all the special triangles, try this problem. Note: Figure not drawn to scale.

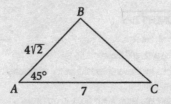

In the triangle on the previous page, what is the length of side BC?

(A) 4

(B) 5

(C) $4\sqrt{2}$

(D) 6

(E) $5\sqrt{2}$        [Answer: B]

You can drop a vertical line from B to line AC. This divides the triangle into two right triangles. That means you know two of the angles in the triangle on the left: 90° and 45°. The third angle must also be 45°, so this is an isosceles right triangle, with sides in the ratio of 1 to 1 to $\sqrt{2}$.

The hypotenuse here is $4\sqrt{2}$, so both legs have length 4. Filling this in, you have the following:

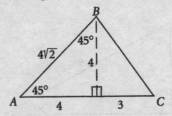

Now you can see that the legs of the smaller triangle on the right must be 4 and 3, making this a 3-4-5 right triangle, and the length of hypotenuse BC is 5. So choice (B) is correct.

---

## BASIC MATH CONCEPT TIPS

Averages—Work with the sum.

Ratios—Identify the parts and the whole.

Rates—Pick numbers for the variables to make the relationship between units clear.

Percents—Make sure you know which whole to plug in.

Simultaneous equations—Combine equations by adding or subtracting them to cancel out all but one variable.

Special triangles—Look for special triangles in geometry problems.

## Multiple and Strange Figures

In a problem that combines figures, you have to look for the relationship between the figures. Look for pieces the figures have in common. For instance, if two figures share a side, information about that side will probably be the key.

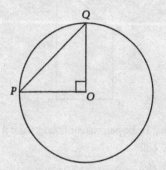

In the figure above, if the area of the circle with center $O$ is $9\pi$, what is the area of triangle $POQ$?

(A) 4.5

(B) 6

(C) 9

(D) $3.5\pi$

(E) $4.5\pi$ [Answer: A]

In this case, the figures don't share a side, but the triangle's legs are important features of the circle—they are radii. You can see that $PO = OQ =$ the radius of circle $O$. The area of the circle is $9\pi$. The area of a circle is $\pi r^2$, where $r =$ the radius. So $9\pi = \pi r^2$, $9 = r^2$, and the radius $= 3$.

The area of a triangle is $\left(\dfrac{1}{2}\right)$ base × height. Therefore, the area of $\triangle POQ$ is $\dfrac{1}{2}(\text{leg}_1 \times \text{leg}_2) = \dfrac{1}{2}(3 \times 3) = \dfrac{9}{2} = 4.5$, answer choice (A).

But what if, instead of a number of familiar shapes, you are given something like this?

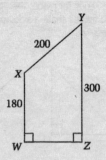

What is the perimeter of quadrilateral *WXYZ*?

(A) 680

(B) 760

(C) 840

(D) 920

(E) 1,000            [Answer: C]

Try breaking the unfamiliar shape into familiar ones. Once this is done, you can use the same techniques that you would for multiple figures. Perimeter is the sum of the lengths of the sides of a figure, so you need to find the length of *WZ*. Drawing a perpendicular line from point *X* to side *YZ* will divide the figure into a right triangle and a rectangle. Call the point of intersection *A*.

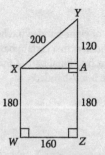

Opposite sides of a rectangle have equal length, so $WZ = XA$ and $WX = ZA$. $WX$ is labeled as 180, so $ZA = 180$. Because $YZ$ measures 300, $AY$ is $300 - 180 = 120$. In right triangle $XYA$, hypotenuse $XY = 200$, and leg $AY = 120$; you should recognize this as a multiple of a 3-4-5 right triangle. The hypotenuse is $5 \times 40$, one leg is $3 \times 40$, so $XA$ must be $4 \times 40$ or 160. (If you didn't recognize this special right triangle, you could have used the Pythagorean theorem to find the length of $XA$.) Because $WZ = XA = 160$, the perimeter of the figure is $180 + 200 + 300 + 160 = 840$, answer choice (C).

## PRACTICE

We have labeled the following questions by the math concept they test. If you get stumped, go back to the appropriate part of this chapter and refresh your memory on how to solve that kind of problem. There is no time limit for this practice set. Answers and explanations are found on page 109.

### Remainders

1. When $z$ is divided by 8, the remainder is 5.
   What is the remainder when $4z$ is divided by 8?

   (A) 1

   (B) 3

   (C) 4

   (D) 5

   (E) 7

## Ratios

2. The ratio of right-handed pitchers to left-handed pitchers in a certain baseball league is 11:7. What fractional part of the pitchers in the league is left-handed?

   (A) $\dfrac{6}{7}$

   (B) $\dfrac{6}{11}$

   (C) $\dfrac{7}{11}$

   (D) $\dfrac{7}{18}$

   (E) $\dfrac{11}{18}$

## Symbols

3. If $x \neq 0$, let $\neg x$ be defined by $\neg x = x - \dfrac{1}{x}$. What is the value of $\neg 2 - \neg \dfrac{1}{2}$?

## Combinations

4. A three-digit code is made up of three different digits from the set {2, 4, 6, 8}. If 2 is always the first digit in the code, how many three-digit codes can be formed if each digit is used only once?

(A) 6

(B) 8

(C) 10

(D) 12

(E) 16

## Averages

5. The average (arithmetic mean) of six numbers is 16. If five of the numbers are 15, 37, 16, 9, and 23, what is the sixth number?

(A) −4

(B) 0

(C) 6

(D) 16

(E) 20

## Multiple and Strange Figures

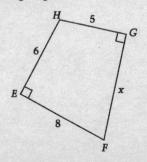

6.  What is the value of $x$ in the figure on the previous page?

    (A) 4

    (B) $3\sqrt{3}$

    (C) $3\sqrt{5}$

    (D) $5\sqrt{3}$

    (E) 9

## Rates

7.  If David paints at the rate of $h$ houses per day, how many houses does he paint in $d$ days, in terms of $h$ and $d$?

    (A) $\dfrac{h}{d}$

    (B) $hd$

    (C) $h + \dfrac{d}{2}$

    (D) $h - d$

    (E) $\dfrac{d}{h}$

## Percents

8.  What is 25 percent of 25 percent of 72?

## Simultaneous Equations

9. If $x + y = 8$ and $y - x = -2$, then $y =$

(A) $-2$

(B) 3

(C) 5

(D) 8

(E) 10

## Special Triangles

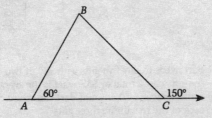

Note: Figure not drawn to scale.

10. In triangle $ABC$ above, if $AB = 4$, then $AC =$

(A) 6

(B) 7

(C) 8

(D) 9

(E) 10

## Remainders

11. When $n$ is divided by 12, the remainder is 0. What is the remainder when $2n$ is divided by 6?

## Averages

12. Bart needs to buy five gifts with $80. If two of the gifts cost a total of $35, what is the average (arithmetic mean) amount Bart can spend on each of the remaining three gifts?

    (A) $10
    (B) $15
    (C) $16
    (D) $17
    (E) $45

## Ratios

13. In a group of 24 people who are either home-owners or renters, the ratio of homeowners to renters is 5:3. How many homeowners are in the group?

    (A) 8
    (B) 9
    (C) 12
    (D) 14
    (E) 15

## Rates

14. Bill has to type a paper that is $p$ pages long, with each page containing $w$ words. If Bill types an average of $x$ words per minute, how many hours will it take him to finish the paper?

   (A) $60wpx$

   (B) $\dfrac{wx}{60p}$

   (C) $\dfrac{60wp}{x}$

   (D) $\dfrac{wpx}{60}$

   (E) $\dfrac{wp}{60x}$

## Percents

15. Eighty-five percent of the members of a student organization registered to attend a field trip. If 16 of the members who registered were unable to attend, resulting in only 65 percent of the members making the trip, how many members are in the organization?

## Special Triangles

16. In the coordinate plane, point $R$ has coordinates $(0, 0)$ and point $S$ has coordinates $(9, 12)$. What is the distance from $R$ to $S$?

## Simultaneous Equations

17. If $4a + 3b = 19$ and $a + 2b = 6$, then $a + b =$

## Symbols

18. If $r \heartsuit s = r(r - s)$ for all integers $r$ and $s$, then
    $4 \heartsuit (3 \heartsuit 5)$ equals

    (A) −8

    (B) −2

    (C) 2

    (D) 20

    (E) 40

## Combinations

19. Five people attend a meeting. If each person
    shakes hands once with every other person at
    the meeting, what is the total number of
    handshakes that take place?

## Multiple and Strange Figures

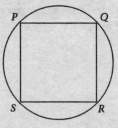

20. In the figure above, square *PQRS* is inscribed in a circle. If the area of square *PQRS* is 4, what is the radius of the circle?

(A) 1

(B) $\sqrt{2}$

(C) 2

(D) $2\sqrt{2}$

(E) $4\sqrt{2}$

## REMEMBER . . .

The SAT tests certain basic skills over and over again. They are:

- Remainders
- Averages
- Ratios
- Rates
- Percents
- Combinations
- Simultaneous Equations
- Symbols
- Special Triangles
- Multiple and Strange Figures

## ANSWERS AND EXPLANATIONS

### Remainders

**1. C**

Let $z = 13$ and plug in $4z = 4(13) = 52$, which leaves a remainder of 4 when divided by 8.

### Ratios

**2. D**

The parts are the number of right-handed (11) and the number of left-handed pitchers (7). The whole is the total number of pitchers (right-handed + left-handed), which is $11 + 7$, or 18. So:

$$\frac{\text{part}}{\text{whole}} = \frac{\text{left-handed}}{\text{total}} = \frac{7}{11 + 7} = \frac{7}{18}.$$

### Symbols

**3. 3**

Identify the value of $\neg 2$ and then of $\neg \frac{1}{2}$, and then subtract the second value from the first:

$$\neg 2 = 2 - \frac{1}{2} = 1\frac{1}{2} = \frac{3}{2}$$

$$\neg \frac{1}{2} = \frac{1}{2} - \frac{1}{\frac{1}{2}} = \frac{1}{2} - 2 = -1\frac{1}{2} = -\frac{3}{2}$$

$$\neg 2 - \neg \frac{1}{2} = \frac{3}{2} - \left(-\frac{3}{2}\right) = \frac{3}{2} + \frac{3}{2} = \frac{6}{2} = 3$$

### Combinations

**4. A**

Every code starts with 2, so the last two digits determine the number of possibilities. The last two digits could be: 46, 48, 64, 68, 84, and 86. That makes six combinations that fit the conditions.

## Averages

**5. A**

Average × Number of Terms = Sum of Terms

$16 \times 6 = 15 + 37 + 16 + 9 + 23 + x$

$96 = 100 + x$

$-4 = x$

## Multiple and Strange Figures

**6. D**

Draw a straight line from point H to point F to divide the figure into two right triangles.

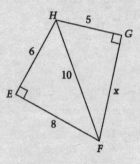

$\triangle EFH$ is a 3-4-5 right triangle with a hypotenuse of length 10. Use the Pythagorean theorem in $\triangle FGH$ to find $x$:

$x^2 + 5^2 = 10^2$

$x^2 + 25 = 100$

$x^2 = 75$

$x = \sqrt{75}$

$x = \sqrt{25}(\sqrt{3})$

$x = 5\sqrt{3}$

## Rates

### 7. B

Pick numbers for $h$ and $d$. Let $h = 2$ and $d = 3$; that is, suppose he paints two houses per day and he paints for three days, so in three days he can paint six houses. You multiply the rate ($h$) by the number of days ($d$). The only answer choice that equals 6 when $h = 2$ and $d = 3$ is choice (B).

## Percents

### 8. 4.5

"25 percent of 25 percent" means $(.25)(.25)$, so $(.25)(.25)(72) = 4.5$.

## Simultaneous Equations

### 9. B

When you add the two equations, the $x$s cancel out and you find that $2y = 6$, so $y = 3$.

## Special Triangles

### 10. C

Angle $BCA$ is supplementary to the angle marked $150°$, so angle $BCA = 180° - 150° = 30°$. Because the sum of interior angles of a triangle is $180°$, angle $A$ + angle $B$ + angle $BCA = 180°$, so angle $B = 180° - 60° - 30° = 90°$. So, triangle $ABC$ is a 30-60-90 triangle, and its sides are in the ratio 1:2. The side opposite the $30°$, $AB$, which we know has length 4, must be half the length of the hypotenuse, $AC$. Therefore, $AC = 8$, and that's answer choice (C).

## Remainders

### 11. 0

If there's no remainder when $n$ is divided by 12, then $n$ is a multiple of 12, as is $2n$. Anything that's a multiple of 12 is a multiple of factors of 12, so $2n$ is a multiple of 6. Thus, the remainder is 0 when $2n$ is divided by 6. Picking numbers highlights this. Say $n$ is 24. $2n$ is 48, and there's a remainder of 0 when 48 is divided by 6.

## Averages

### 12. B

Bart has $80 and spent $35 on two gifts; therefore, he has $45 left to spend on the remaining three. So,

$$x = \frac{\$45}{3}$$

$$x = \$15$$

## Ratios

### 13. E

The parts are the number of homeowners (5) and the number of renters (3). The whole is the total (homeowners + renters).

So: $\dfrac{\text{part}}{\text{whole}} = \dfrac{\text{homeowners}}{\text{homeowners} + \text{renters}} = \dfrac{5}{5+3} = \dfrac{5}{8}$.

Because there are 24 people in the group, $= \dfrac{5}{8} = \dfrac{x}{24}$ making $x = 15$.

## Rates

### 14. E

Pick numbers for $p$, $w$, and $x$ that work well in the problem. Let $p = 3$ and let $w = 100$. So there are three pages with 100 words per page, or 300 words total. Say he types five words a minute, so $x = 5$. Therefore, he types $5 \times 60$, or 300 words an hour. It takes him one hour to type the paper. The only answer choice that equals 1 when $p = 3$, $w = 100$, and $x = 5$ is choice (E).

## Percents

### 15. 80

You need to solve for the whole, so identify the part and the percent. If 85 percent planned to attend and only 65 percent did, 20 percent failed to attend, and you know that 16 students failed to attend.

Percent × Whole = Part

$$\frac{20}{100} \times \text{Whole} = 16$$

$$\text{Whole} = 16 \times \frac{100}{20}$$

$$\text{Whole} = 80$$

## Special Triangles

### 16. 15

Draw a diagram. Because RS isn't parallel to either axis, the way to compute its length is to create a right triangle with legs that are parallel to the axes, so their lengths are easy to find. If the triangle formed is not a special triangle, we can then use the Pythagorean theorem to find the length of RS.

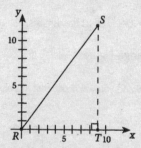

Because S has a y-coordinate of 12, it's 12 units above the x-axis, so the length of ST must be 12. Also, because T is the same number of units to the right of the y-axis as S, given by the x-coordinate of 9, the distance from the origin to T must be 9. So we have a right triangle with legs of 9 and 12. You should recognize this as a multiple of the 3-4-5 triangle; $9 = 3 \times 3$; $12 = 3 \times 4$; so the hypotenuse RS must be $3 \times 5$, or 15.

## Simultaneous Equations

### 17. 5

Adding the two equations, you find that $5a + 5b = 25$. Dividing by 5 shows that $a + b = 5$.

## Symbols

### 18. E

Start in the parentheses and work out: $(3 \heartsuit 5) = 3(3 - 5) =$
$3(-2) = -6$; $4 \heartsuit (-6) = 4[4 - (-6)] = 4(10) = 40$.

## Combinations

### 19. 10

Be careful not to count each handshake twice. Call the five people A, B, C, D, and E. We can pair them off like this:

A with B, C, D, and E (four handshakes)

B with C, D, and E (three more—note that we leave out A because the handshake between A and B is already counted)

C with D and E (two more)

D with E (one more)

The total is $4 + 3 + 2 + 1$, or 10 handshakes.

## Multiple and Strange Figures

### 20. B

Draw in diagonal $QS$ and you will notice that it is also a diameter of the circle.

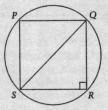

Because the area of the square is 4, its sides must each be 2. Think of the diagonal as dividing the square into two isosceles right triangles. Therefore, the diagonal $= 2\sqrt{2} =$ the diameter; the radius is half this amount, or $\sqrt{2}$.

# Chapter Six: Advanced SAT Math Concepts

- Advanced Math Topics
- Advanced Math Tips
- Advanced Math Practice

One of the big changes in the new SAT is the addition of more and harder math. If you had been born just a few years earlier, you would have taken an SAT that tested only basic math. But, alas, this is the SAT you are taking, so we must prepare you for the more difficult math.

## ADVANCED MATH TOPICS

All 20 of these advanced math topics are now fair game on the New SAT:

1. Sequences involving exponential growth
2. Sets
3. Absolute value
4. Rational equations and inequalities
5. Radical equations
6. Manipulation with integer and rational exponents
7. Direct and inverse variation
8. Function notation and evaluation
9. Concepts of domain and range
10. Functions as models
11. Linear functions—equations and graphs
12. Quadratic functions—equations and graphs

13. Geometric notation
14. Trigonometry as an alternative method of solution
15. Properties of tangent lines
16. Coordinate geometry
17. Qualitative behavior of graphs and functions
18. Transformations and their effect on graphs and functions
19. Data interpretation, scatterplots, and matrices
20. Geometric probability

This chapter introduces you to these concepts and shows you how the SAT is likely to test them. (Remember, they haven't tested them yet, so we are providing you with the ways our research and experience lead us to believe they will test these concepts.)

## Sequences Involving Exponential Growth

The name sounds like a mouthful, but relax: sequences involving exponential growth, also known as geometric sequences, are a tough but manageable area of SAT math.

What is a geometric sequence, and what does it take to ace questions about them on the SAT? A geometric sequence of numbers is simply one in which a constant ratio exists between consecutive terms. Questions about geometric sequences are likely to hinge on this formula:

If $r$ is the ratio between consecutive terms, $a_1$ is the first term, and $a_n$ is the $n$th term, then $a_n = a_1 r^{n-1}$

This is how the SAT might ask a question about geometric sequences.

> If the first term in a geometric sequence is 4, and the fifth term is 64, what is the eighth term?
>
> (A)  512
>
> (B)  864
>
> (C)  1,245
>
> (D)  13,404
>
> (E)  22,682                    [Answer: A]

First, use the formula to solve for $r$:

$64 = 4r^4$

$16 = r^4$

$r = 2$

Now, using $r = 2$, solve for $a_8$:

$a_8 = 4(2)^7$

$a_8 = 512$

If $r$ is the ratio between consecutive terms, $a_1$ is the first term, and $a_n$ is the $n$th term, then $a_n = a_1 r^{n-1}$.

## Sets

The things in a set are called *elements* or *members*. The union of sets, sometimes expressed with the symbol ∪, is the set of elements that are in either or both of the different sets you start with. Think of the union set as what you get when you merge sets. For example, if Set $A = \{1, 2\}$ and Set $B = \{3, 4\}$, then $A ∪ B \{1, 2, 3, 4\}$.

The intersection of sets, sometimes expressed with the symbol ∩, is the set of elements common to the respective sets you start with. For example, if Set $A = \{1, 2, 3\}$ and Set $B = \{3, 4, 5\}$, then $A ∩ B = \{3\}$.

Try to work through the following example.

> If Set $R$ contains 6 distinct numbers and Set $S$ contains 5 distinct letters, how many elements are in the union of the two sets?
>
> (A)  1
>
> (B)  5
>
> (C)  6
>
> (D)  8
>
> (E)  11                                  [Answer: E]

Because Set $R$ and Set $S$ contain different kinds of elements, no element is in both sets. So the union set of $S$ and $R$—$S ∪ R$—contains everything in each: $6 + 5 = 11$.

### SETS

Think of the union of sets as what you get when you merge the sets.
Think of the intersection of sets as the overlap of the sets.

## Absolute Value

The absolute value of a number is the distance between that number
and zero on the number line. Because absolute value is a distance, it
is always positive. The absolute value of 7 is 7; this is expressed as
$|7| = 7$. Similarly, the absolute value of $-7$ is 7: $|-7| = 7$. Every positive number is the absolute value of two numbers: itself and its negative counterpart. As you'll see in the next example, the SAT sometimes connects the concept of absolute value to the concept of
inequalities.

> If $|r + 7| < 2$, which of the following
> statements are true?
>
> I. $r < -9$
> II. $r < -5$
> III. $r > -9$
>
> (A) I only
> (B) II only
> (C) III only
> (D) I and II only
> (E) II and III only         [Answer: E]

You can solve this problem algebraically, as shown below, or you can
think about what the inequality would look like on a number line. You
can express $|r + 7| < 2$ *as the difference between r and –7 is less
than 2* and determine that *r* must be between –5 and –9:

$r + 7 < 2$ and $-r - 7 < 2$

$r < -5$ and $-r < 9$

$r < -5$ and $r > -9$

---

ABSOLUTE VALUE

The distance of a number from zero on the number line.

## Rational Equations and Inequalities

A rational equation or inequality is one that contains at least one fraction in which the numerator and denominator are polynomials.

> For all values of $x$ not equal to $-2$ or $3$,
> $$\frac{x^4 - 5x^3 - 2x^2 + 24x}{x^2 - x - 6}$$ is equal to
>
> (A) $x^2 - 4x$
> (B) $x^2 - 5x - 2$
> (C) $x + 24$
> (D) $x$
> (E) $x - 4$ [Answer: A]

Picking numbers is the easiest way to solve this problem. Say $x = 2$:

$$\frac{2^4 - 5(2^3) - 2(2^2) + 24(2)}{2^2 - 2 - 6} = \frac{16 - 5(8) - 2(4) + 24(2)}{4 - 2 - 6} =$$

$$\frac{16 - 40 - 8 + 48}{-4} = \frac{16}{-4} = -4$$

Now find the choice that has a value of $-4$ when $x = 2$. Only (A) works: $2^2 - 4(2) = 4 - 8 = -4$. So, (A) is the correct answer.

## Radical Equations

Like rational equations, radical equations—ones with at least one variable under a radical sign—follow the same rules as other kinds of algebraic equations, so solve them accordingly. What makes radical equations special is that the last step in isolating the variable is often to square both sides of the equation. Look at the following example.

> If $4 - \sqrt{n} = -1$, what is the value of $n$?
> (A) 3
> (B) 5
> (C) 9
> (D) 25
> (E) 81 [Answer: D]

Apply the same algebraic steps here as you would in any other question involving an equation, isolating the variable step by step. Just remember to square both sides of the equation as your last step. (Notice that (B) is a trap set for test takers who forget to do so. We will cover math traps in more detail in the next chapter.)

$$4 - \sqrt{n} = -1$$
$$5 = \sqrt{n}$$
$$(5)^2 = (\sqrt{n})^2$$
$$25 = n$$

## Manipulation with Integer and Rational Exponents

Not every exponent on the SAT is a positive integer. Numbers can be raised to a fractional or negative exponent. Although such numbers follow their own special rules, they adhere to the same general rules of exponents that you've probably worked with before.

$$\text{If } x = \frac{1}{4}, x^{-4} =$$

(A) $\dfrac{-1}{256}$

(B) $\dfrac{-1}{16}$

(C) $\quad 4$

(D) $\quad 16$

(E) $\quad 256$            [Answer: E]

To find the value of a number raised to a negative power, simply rewrite the number, without the negative sign in front of the exponent, as the bottom of a fraction with 1 as the numerator of the fraction: $3^{-2} = \dfrac{1}{3^2} = \dfrac{1}{9}$. In this case:

$$x^{-4} = \frac{1}{x^4} = \frac{1}{(\frac{1}{4})^4} = \frac{1}{(\frac{1}{256})} = 256.$$

## Direct and Inverse Variation

In direct variation, $y = kx$, where $k$ is a nonzero constant. In direct variation, the variable $y$ changes directly as $x$ does. If a unit of Currency $A$ is worth 2 units of Currency $B$, then $A = 2B$. If the number of units of $B$ were to double, the number of units of $A$ would double, and so on for halving, tripling, etc.

In inverse variation, $xy = k$, where $x$ and $y$ are variables and $k$ is a constant. A famous inverse relationship is *rate × time = distance*. Imagine having to cover a distance of 24 miles. If you were to travel at 12 miles per hour, you'd need 2 hours. But if you were to cut your rate in half, you would have to double your time. This is just another way of saying that rate and time vary inversely. The following is an example of direct and indirect variation.

> If the length of a sea turtle is directly proportional to its age, and a 2-year-old sea turtle is 3 inches long, how many feet long is an 80-year-old sea turtle?
>
> (A) 10
>
> (B) 12
>
> (C) 100
>
> (D) 120
>
> (E) 144 [Answer: A]

Relate the length of the turtle to its age. Use the equation to find the length of an 80-year-old sea turtle in inches; then convert from inches to feet. Because length is directly proportional to age, you can represent their relationship as $l = ka$, where $l$ is length, $a$ is age, and $k$ is a constant:

$3 = k(2)$

$1.5 = k$

$l = 1.5(80) = 120$ inches $= 10$ feet

(A) is the correct answer.

## Function Notation and Evaluation

A few questions on Test Day will probably focus on functions and use standard function notation such as $f(x)$. Evaluating a function sounds fancy, but it mostly involves substitution of numbers for variables—a skill you should already be familiar with.

For example, to evaluate the function $f(x) = 5x + 1$ for $f(3)$, replace $x$ with 3 and simplify: $f(3) = 5(3) + 1 = 15 + 1 = 16$

The example below presents a slightly more complex variation: a composition of functions. $h[g(a)]$ requires you to first evaluate $g(a)$, and then apply $h$ to the result.

> If $g(a) = (a + 4)^2$ and $h(b) = 2b - 7$, then
> what is the value of $h[g(2)]$?
>
> (A) 1
> (B) 36
> (C) 45
> (D) 65
> (E) 79                              [Answer: D]

Follow the order of operations:

$g(2) = (2 + 4)^2 = 6^2 = 36$

$h(36) = 2(36) - 7 = 72 - 7 = 65$

## Concepts of Domain and Range

The domain of a function is the set of values for which the function is defined. For example, the domain of $f(x) = \dfrac{1}{1 - x^2}$ is all values of $x$ except 1 and −1, because for those values, the denominator has a value of 0 and is therefore undefined. The range of a function is the set of outputs or results of the function. For example, the range of $f(x) = x^2$ is all numbers greater than or equal to zero because $x^2$ cannot be negative. Try the following sample question.

If $f(a) = a^2 + 7$ for all real values of $a$, which of the following is a possible value of $f(a)$?

(A) −2

(B) 0

(C) $\sqrt{5}$

(D) $\sqrt{7}$

(E) $100\sqrt{3}$           [Answer: E]

If $a$ is a real number, then $a^2$ must be positive or equal to zero. Think about how this limits the range of $f(a)$: If $a = 0$, then $f(a) = 7$. All other values of $a$ result in a higher value of $f(a)$. Only (E) is greater than 7.

---

### FUNCTIONS

The domain of a function is the set of values for which the function is defined. The range of a function is the set of possible values of the function.

## Functions as Models

The SAT might challenge your ability to relate functional relationships to real-life situations. For example, you may be asked to interpret data about the relationship between the selling price of a car and the number of cars that sell at that price.

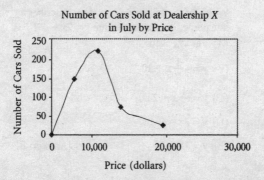

Number of Cars Sold at Dealership X
in July by Price

The graph on the previous page represents the number of cars sold at Dealership $X$ in July. If the dealer wants to sell the maximum number of cars possible in August, at what price should he set the cars, based on his sales in July?

(A)  5,000

(B)  10,000

(C)  15,000

(D)  20,000

(E)  22,500                           [Answer: B]

Make sure to read your graphs carefully, knowing what each axis represents. If you are not careful, you may choose the incorrect answer that is meant as a trap.

Use the graph of July to figure out which price point sold the most cars. The peak value is $10,000, which sold 225 cars. Based on this information, the dealer should price cars at $10,000 in August and hope to sell the maximum number of cars that he can in that month.

## Linear Functions—Equations and Graphs

You'll most likely see a question or two on the SAT involving equations and graphs of linear functions. A linear function is simply an equation whose graph is a straight line. For example:

Which of the following equations describes a line perpendicular to the line $y = 7x + 49$?

(A) $y = -7x - 49$

(B) $y = -\dfrac{1}{7}x + 10$

(C) $y = \dfrac{1}{7}x + 7$

(D) $y = 7x - 49$

(E) $y = 7x + 14$                      [Answer: B]

If two lines are perpendicular, then the slope of one is the negative reciprocal of the slope of the other. These lines are written in the form $y = mx + b$, where $m$ is the slope and $b$ is the y-intercept, or the value of $y$ when $x = 0$. In this case, the negative reciprocal of 7 is $-\frac{1}{7}$. The only equation with this slope is (B).

---

**SLOPES**

Parallel lines have equal slopes. Perpendicular lines have negative reciprocal slopes.

## Quadratic Functions—Equations and Graphs

A quadratic function is one that takes the form $f(x) = ax^2 + bx + c$. Rather than take the form of a straight line as, you'll recall, a linear function does, the graph of a quadratic function is a parabola. As the question next illustrates, a quadratic function question could be similar to a quadratic equations question.

> If $x^2 - 7x + 12 = 0$, what is the sum of the
> two possible values of $x$ ?
>
> (A) −4
>
> (B) −1
>
> (C) 3
>
> (D) 4
>
> (E) 7                                      [Answer: C]

Factor:

$x^2 - 7x + 12 = 0$

$(x - 4)(x - 3) = 0$

$x = 4$ or $x = 3$

$4 + 3 = 7$

## Geometric Notation for Length, Segments, Lines, Rays, and Congruence

You should expect SAT geometry questions to use the symbols $\leftrightarrow$, $\overline{\phantom{--}}$, and $\cong$.

$\leftrightarrow$ signifies a line. $\overleftrightarrow{XY}$ is the line that passes through points $X$ and $Y$.

$\overline{\phantom{--}}$ signifies line segment: $\overline{XY}$ is the line segment whose endpoints are $X$ and $Y$.

$\cong$ symbolizes congruence. If two triangles are congruent, they coincide exactly when superimposed. You may want to think of two congruent figures as identical twins.

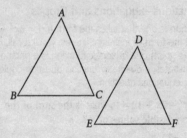

Note: Figures not drawn to scale.

$\angle CAB \cong \angle FDE$ and $\angle ABC \cong \angle DEF$. Which of the following must be true?

I. $\cup ABC \cong \cup DEF$
II. Triangles $ABC$ and $DEF$ are similar.
III. $\overline{AB} = \overline{DE}$

(A) II only
(B) III only
(C) I and III
(D) II and III
(E) I, II, and III                    [Answer: A]

When a figure is not drawn to scale, it is most likely drawn in a misleading way. This figure certainly looks as though *ABC* and *DEF* are identical and that all their parts are congruent, but you can't assume that based on the information in the problem. You may want to draw your own diagrams to think about some of the different possibilities. All we know about these triangles is that they share two angles. Therefore, the third angle of each triangle must also be congruent. This tells us that the triangles are similar because their angles are the same. However, we know nothing about the lengths of the sides—one triangle could be much smaller than the other; thus, choice (A) is the correct answer.

## Trigonometry as an Alternative Method of Solution

Now more than ever, the SAT will reward test takers who recall the special relationships in 45-45-90 and 30-60-90 right triangles:

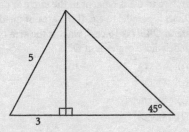

What is the total area of this figure above?

To find the area of a triangle, you need its height and the length of its base. Think about the information presented in the figure. What other data can you derive from it? The triangle on the left is a special triangle with side lengths of 3, 4, and 5. (You could also find the missing side using the Pythagorean theorem.) The triangle on the right is a 45-45-90 triangle, so its base must also equal 4. The total area of the figure is $\frac{1}{2}(3 + 4)(4) = 14$.

## Properties of Tangent Lines

When a line is tangent to a circle, the radius of the circle is perpendicular to the line at the point of contact. Look at the following example.

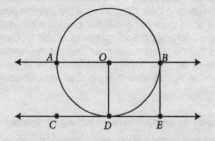

In the figure above, $\overleftrightarrow{AB}$ is a diameter of the circle, and $\overleftrightarrow{CE}$ is tangent to the circle at point $D$. $\overleftrightarrow{AB}$ is parallel to $\overleftrightarrow{CE}$. If the area of quadrilateral $OBED$ is 16 cm$^2$, what is the area of the circle whose center is at $O$?

(A)    4 cm$^2$

(B)    $4\pi$ cm$^2$

(C)    $8\pi$ cm$^2$

(D)   $16\pi$ cm$^2$

(E)   256 cm$^2$                    [Answer: D]

Because there's a circle in this problem, you can be sure you'll need the radius at some point. To figure out how to get that from the area of quadrilateral $OBED$, you'll need to use the rest of the information in the question stem. It may be helpful to add a few angles to the figure—for instance, because $\overleftrightarrow{CE}$ is tangent to the circle at point $D$, it is perpendicular to the radius of the circle at that point. The information given in the first two sentences of the question stem tells you that $\overline{OD}$ is perpendicular to $\overleftrightarrow{CE}$ and therefore also to $\overleftrightarrow{AB}$. $\overline{OD}$ and $\overline{OB}$ are both radii of the circle, so quadrilateral $OBED$ is a square. The area of $OBED$ is 16, so each side has a length of 4. This is also the radius of the circle. $4^2\pi = 16\pi$ is the area of the circle, so you should have chosen answer (D).

## Coordinate Geometry

Coordinate geometry questions on the SAT tend to focus on the properties of straight lines. The equation of a straight line is $y = mx + b$, where $y$ and $x$ are the infinite number of coordinated $(x, y)$ pairs that fall on the line. $b$ is the $y$-intercept, or the value of $y$ when $x = 0$. $m$ is the slope of the line and is expressed, $\frac{\Delta Y}{\Delta X}$, or $\frac{y_2 - y_1}{x_2 - x_1}$. What this means, exactly, is that the slope or steepness of a line is the change in $y$-values in relation to the change in corresponding $x$-values. Positive slopes tilt upward to the right. Negative slopes tilt downward to the right. A horizontal line has a slope of zero. A vertical line has an undefined slope. Parallel lines have equal slopes. Perpendicular lines have negative reciprocal slopes.

As this question illustrates, the SAT may also ask you to identify the midpoint of a line segment or the distance between two points.

> If point $P$ is at $(8, 10)$ and point $Q$ is at $(0, 4)$, what is the midpoint of $PQ$ ?
>
> (A) $(0, 10)$
> (B) $(4, 2)$
> (C) $(4, 5)$
> (D) $(4, 7)$
> (E) $(9, 2)$ [Answer: D]

The midpoint of a line segment whose ends are at the points $(x_1, y_1)$ and $(x_2, y_2)$ is the point $\left( \dfrac{x_1 + x_2}{2}, \dfrac{y_1 + y_2}{2} \right)$. Now plug in the numbers from the question.

$$x = \frac{8 + 0}{2} = \frac{8}{2} = 4$$

$$y = \frac{10 + 4}{2} = \frac{14}{2} = 7$$

The midpoint is (4, 7).

---

### DISTANCE FORMULA

The distance between the points $(x_1, y_1)$ and $(x_2, y_2)$ is given by the distance formula:
$$\sqrt{(x_2 - x_1)^2 + (y_2 - y_1)^2}.$$

## Qualitative Behavior of Graphs and Functions

The SAT will likely ask you to show an understanding of a general or particular property of a complex graph, such as the one in this example:

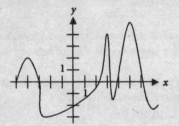

The figure above shows the graph of $f(x)$. At how many values of $x$ does $f(x)$ equal 4?

(A) 0

(B) 1

(C) 2

(D) 3

(E) 4           [Answer: D]

The value of $f(x)$ is measured on the y-axis. Find 4 on the y-axis, and then see how many points on the graph have a y-value of 4. The points are approximately (3, 4), (4.7, 4), and (5.4, 4). So your answer here is 3.

## Transformations and Their Effect on Graphs of Functions

A transformation is an alteration in a function. An SAT question might present a graph and ask you to identify a specific transformation, such as in the following question.

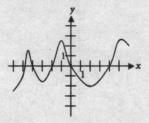

The figure above shows the graph of the function $r(x)$. Which of the following figures shows the graph of the function $r(x - 2)$?

(A)

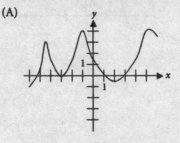

(B)

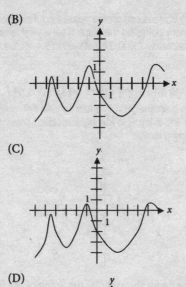

(C)

(D)

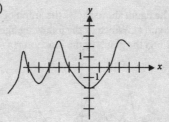

(E)

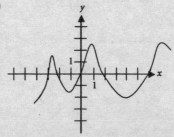

The graph of $r(x - 2)$ will look like the graph of $r(x)$ shifted two units to the right. You can check this by plugging in a few points. For example, $r(-1) = 2.5$, so $r(1 - 2)$ should equal 2.5. This is only true of answer (E).

## Data Interpretation, Scatterplots, and Matrices

Some SAT questions focus on the test taker's ability to interpret, evaluate, and draw conclusions from data presented in matrices or, like those below, in scatterplots.

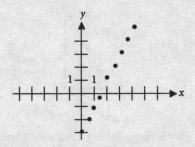

Which of the following equations best fits these points?

(A) $y = 3x + 2$

(B) $y = 3x - 2$

(C) $y = 2x + 3$

(D) $y = 2x - 3$

(E) $y = x - 3$          [Answer: D]

Try to figure out what sort of line would fit these points. What should the slope be? What should the y-intercept be? Remember that the standard equation for a line is in the form $y = mx + b$, where $m$ is the slope and $b$ is the y-intercept.

If you think visually, you might want to try sketching the line described by each answer choice to see which one fits the closest to the points on the graph. If you're more comfortable working with numbers, you could try plugging a few points from the graph into each possible equation to see which one works. The y-intercept of this graph is at −3. The slope is around 2 because the graph is raised about 2 units for every 1 unit it moves along the x-axis.

## Geometric Probability

Geometric probability questions ask you to calculate a probability. At this final stage, use the formula: probability = $\dfrac{\text{desired outcome}}{\text{possible outcome}}$.

Try this formula on the following question.

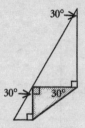

**What is the probability that a point selected at random from the interior of the figure above will fall within the shaded region?**

(A) $\dfrac{\sqrt{3}}{13}$

(B) $\dfrac{3}{13}$

(C) $\dfrac{6}{13}$

(D) $\dfrac{1}{3}$

(E) $\dfrac{1}{2}$ [Answer: B]

The probability that a randomly selected point will fall into the shaded region is equal to the area of the shaded region divided by the area of the entire figure. The figure is made up of three 30-60-90 triangles, so you can calculate the ratio of the lengths of the bases and heights of the various triangles and then find their areas.

This will be easier if you pick a number to be the length of the base of the smallest triangle. The lengths of the sides of a 30-60-90 triangle are in the ratio $x : x\sqrt{3} : 2x$. If the length of the smallest triangle is 1, its height is $\sqrt{3}$. This is also the length of the base of the middle triangle. The height of the middle triangle is $\sqrt{3} \times \sqrt{3} = 3$, which is also the length of the base of the largest triangle. The height of the largest triangle is $3\sqrt{3}$.

Area of smallest triangle: $\dfrac{1}{2}(1)(\sqrt{3}) = \dfrac{\sqrt{3}}{2}$

Area of middle triangle: $\dfrac{1}{2}(\sqrt{3})(3) = \dfrac{3\sqrt{3}}{2}$

Area of largest triangle: $\dfrac{1}{2}(3)(3\sqrt{3}) = \dfrac{9\sqrt{3}}{2}$

Probability $= \dfrac{\text{desired outcome}}{\text{possible outcomes}}$

Probability that a point will lie in the shaded region:

$$\dfrac{\dfrac{3\sqrt{3}}{2}}{\dfrac{3\sqrt{3}}{2} + \dfrac{3\sqrt{3}}{2} + \dfrac{9\sqrt{3}}{2}} = \dfrac{\dfrac{3\sqrt{3}}{2}}{\dfrac{13\sqrt{3}}{2}} = \dfrac{3}{13}$$

## Remember

The new SAT tests more advanced math than the old SATs.

The new SAT tests the following concepts:

- Sequences involving exponential growth
- Sets
- Absolute value
- Rational equations and inequalities
- Radical equations
- Manipulation with integer and rational exponents
- Direct and inverse variation
- Function notation and evaluation
- Concepts of domain and range
- Functions as models
- Linear functions—equations and graphs
- Quadratic functions—equations and graphs
- Geometric notation
- Trigonometry as an alternative method of solution
- Properties of tangent lines
- Coordinate geometry
- Qualitative behavior of graphs and functions
- Transformations and their effect on graphs and functions
- Data interpretation, scatterplots, and matrices
- Geometric probability

## PRACTICE

We have labeled the following questions by the math concept they test. If you get stumped, go back to the appropriate part of this chapter and refresh your memory on how to solve the problem.

### Sequences Involving Exponential Growth

1. A scientist is running an experiment with two species of bacteria that grow exponentially. If species A doubles in population every 2 days, species B doubles in population every 5 days, and each species began the experiment with a population of 50 bacteria, what will the difference be between the populations of the two species after 10 days?

    (A)  200
    (B)  800
    (C) 1,200
    (D) 1,400
    (E) 1,500

### Sets

2. If set $A = \{2, 3, 5, 7, 10\}$ and set $B = \{3, 4, 5, 6, 7\}$, how many elements are in the intersection of the two sets?

    (A)  2
    (B)  3
    (C)  5
    (D)  7
    (E)  10

## Absolute Value

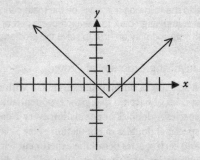

3. Which of the following equations best represents the graph above?

(A) $y = |x|$

(B) $y = |x| - 1$

(C) $y = |x - 1|$

(D) $y = |x - 1| - 1$

(E) $y = |x - 2|$

## Rational Equations and Inequalities

4. If $\dfrac{x^3 - 4x}{x^3 - 5x^2 + 6x} = 0$, and $x \neq 0$, 2, or 3, what is the value of $x$?

(A) −3

(B) −2

(C) 0

(D) 1

(E) 4

## Radical Equations

5. If $\sqrt{x + 2y} - 2 = 15$, what is the value of $y$ in terms of $x$?

   (A) $\dfrac{289 - x}{2}$

   (B) $289 - x$

   (C) $\dfrac{17 - x}{2}$

   (D) $17 - x$

   (E) $289$

## Manipulation with Integer and Rational Exponents

6. What is the value of $4^{\frac{1}{2}} + 4^{\frac{3}{2}}$?

   (A)  4

   (B)  8

   (C) 10

   (D) 16

   (E) 64

## Direct and Inverse Variation

7. The rate at which a balloon travels is inversely proportional to the amount of weight attached to it.  If the balloon travels at 10 inches per second when there is a 2-gram weight attached to it, approximately how much weight must be attached to the balloon for it to travel 18 inches per second?

   (A)  0.4 grams

   (B)  1.0 gram

   (C)  1.1 grams

   (D)  3.6 grams

   (E) 10.0 grams

## Function Notation and Evaluation

8. If $f(x) = \dfrac{(x^2 - 9)}{(x + 3)}$, what is the value of $f(-4)$?

(A) −7

(B) $-\dfrac{1}{4}$

(C) 0

(D) $\dfrac{1}{4}$

(E) 7

## Concepts of Domain and Range

9. If $g(x) = 2 - \sqrt{x - 7}$, and $g(x)$ is a real number, which of the following cannot be the value of $x$?

(A) 4

(B) 7

(C) 11

(D) 102

(E) 496

## Functions as Models

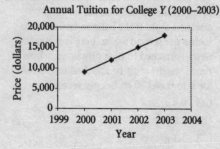

Annual Tuition for College Y (2000–2003)

10. The graph on the previous page represents the annual tuition for college $Y$ from 2000–2003. Based on the graph, what was most likely the tuition for college $Y$ in 1999?

    (A) $6,000

    (B) $9,000

    (C) $15,000

    (D) $18,000

    (E) $21,000

## Linear Functions—Equations and Graphs

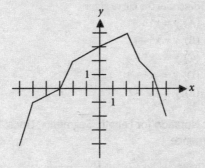

11. The graph shows the function $g(x)$. What is the value of $g(0)$?

    (A) $-1$

    (B) $\dfrac{-1}{2}$

    (C) $0$

    (D) $1$

    (E) $3$

## Quadratic Functions—Equations and Graphs

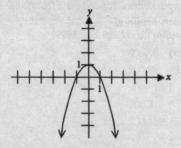

12. Which of the following equations best describes the curve above?

    (A) $y = x^2 + 4$
    (B) $y = x^2 - 1$
    (C) $y = -x^2 + 4$
    (D) $y = -x^2 + 1$
    (E) $y = -x^2 - 1$

## Geometric Notation for Length, Segments, Lines, Rays, and Congruence

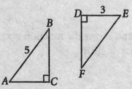

13. In the figure above, $\triangle ABC \cong \triangle EFD$. What is the area of $\triangle ABC$?

    (A)  6
    (B)  7.5
    (C) $6\sqrt{2}$
    (D) $6\sqrt{3}$
    (E)  12

## Trigonometry as an Alternative Method of Solution

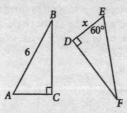

14. In the figure above, $\triangle ABC \cong \triangle EFD$. What is the
    value of $x$?

    (A) 3
    (B) 4
    (C) 5
    (D) 6
    (E) 7

## Properties of Tangent Lines

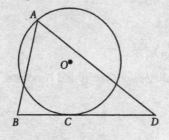

Note: Figure not drawn to scale.

15. In the figure on the previous page, $\overline{BD}$ is 8 units long and is tangent to the circle at point C. $AC$ is a diameter of the circle. If the circumference of the circle is $6\pi$, what is the area of $\triangle ABD$?

   (A)    9
   (B)    12
   (C)    24
   (D)    9$\pi$
   (E)    10$\pi$

## Coordinate Geometry

16. If point R is (2, 4) and point S is (7, 7), what is the length of $\overline{RS}$?

   (A) 2
   (B) $\sqrt{7}$
   (C) $\sqrt{34}$
   (D) 9
   (E) $\sqrt{202}$

## Qualitative Behavior of Graphs and Functions

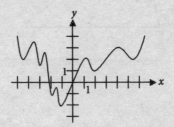

17. The figure on the previous page shows the graph of $g(x)$. What is the largest value of $g(x)$ shown in this figure?

    (A) –2
    (B) 2
    (C) 4
    (D) 6
    (E) 6.5

## Transformations and Their Effect on Graphs of Functions

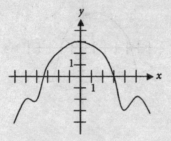

18. The figure above shows the graph of the function $h(x)$. Which of the following figures shows the graph of the function $h(x + 1)$?

    (A)

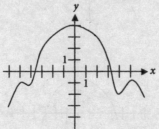

(B)

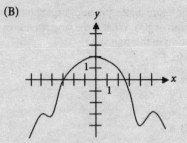

(C)

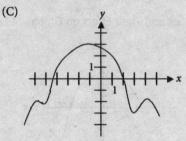

(D)

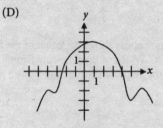

(E)

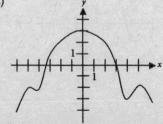

## Data Interpretation, Scatterplots, and Matrices

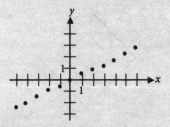

19. Which of the following equations best fits these points?

    (A) $y = \dfrac{1}{2}x$

    (B) $y = \dfrac{1}{2}x + 4$

    (C) $y = x$

    (D) $y = 2x - 4$

    (E) $y = 2x$

## Geometric Probability

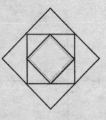

20. The figure above shows a square inscribed in a square inscribed in another square. What is the probability that a point selected at random from the interior of the figure will fall within the shaded region?

(A) $\frac{1}{5}$

(B) $\frac{1}{4}$

(C) $\frac{1}{3}$

(D) $\frac{4}{9}$

(E) $\frac{1}{2}$

## ANSWERS AND EXPLANATIONS

### Sequences Involving Exponential Growth

**1. D**

Both species are growing exponentially, which means that the population at any point in time can be described by the equation $n = n_0 2^{\frac{t}{x}}$, where $n_0$ is the initial population, $t$ is the number of days that have passed since the start of the experiment, and $x$ is the number of days in which the population doubles. You don't have to know this equation to solve the problem—you could just double the original number of bacteria as many times as required to find the population of each species after 10 days, and then find the difference between them:

Population of species A: $(50)2^{\frac{10}{2}} = (50)2^5 = (50)32 = 1,600$

Population of species B: $(50)2^{\frac{10}{5}} = (50)2^2 = (50)4 = 200$

$1,600 - 200 = 1,400.$

### Sets

**2. B**

Focus on the overlap of the sets, which share three numbers: 3, 5, and 7. The correct answer is 3.

### Absolute Value

**3. D**

If you're not sure what these transformations of the graph look like, try plugging a few points from the graph into each equation to see which one is correct. Some good points to try include are (0, 0) and (1, −1).

$|0 - 1| - 1 = 1 - 1 = 0$

$|1 - 1| - 1 = 0 - 1 = -1$

## Rational Equations and Inequalities

**4. B**

In general, try to simplify problems with complex rational equations like this by factoring the numerator and denominator to see whether any parts cancel out. In this case, you need only to focus on the numerator. You know the fraction has a value of zero, so the numerator must equal zero:

$$x^3 - 4x = 0$$

$$x(x^2 - 4) = 0$$

$$x(x - 2)(x + 2) = 0$$

$$x = 0, 2, \text{ or } -2$$

The question stem states that $x \neq 0$ or 2, so the answer must be choice (B), $x = -2$.

## Radical Equations

**5. A**

$$\sqrt{x + 2y} - 2 = 15$$

$$\sqrt{x + 2y} = 17$$

$$(\sqrt{x + 2y})^2 = 17^2$$

$$x + 2y = 289$$

$$2y = 289 - x$$

$$y = \frac{289 - x}{2}$$

This is another example designed to illustrate that squaring both sides is not always the last step.

## Manipulation with Integer and Rational Exponents

**6.   C**

If $x$ is a positive real number and $a$ is a nonzero integer, then $x^{\frac{1}{a}} = \sqrt[a]{x}$.
So $4^{\frac{1}{2}} = \sqrt[2]{4} = 2$. If $p$ and $q$ are integers, then $x^{\frac{p}{q}} = \sqrt[q]{x^p}$. So $4^{\frac{3}{2}} =$
$\sqrt[2]{4^3} = \sqrt{64} = 8$. Therefore, $2 + 8 = 10$, and answer choice (C) is correct.

## Direct and Inverse Variation

**7.   C**

To find the exact amount of weight required, set up a relationship
between the rate the balloon travels and the weight attached to it.
Because these quantities vary inversely, you can express that relationship as $h = \dfrac{k}{w}$, where $h$ is the rate of travel of the balloon, $w$ is the
weight attached to it, and $k$ is a constant. First, use the given values of
$h$ and $w$ to find $k$, and then use the equation to find the amount of
weight required to make the balloon travel at 18 inches per second.

$$10 = \frac{k}{2}$$
$$k = 20$$
$$18 = \frac{20}{w}$$

$$w = \frac{20}{18} = \frac{10}{9} = 1.\overline{11}, \text{ which is approximately } 1.1.$$

## Function Notation and Evaluation

**8.   A**

Substitute $-4$ wherever you see $x$:

$$f(x) = \frac{(x^2 - 9)}{(x + 3)}$$

$$f(-4) = \frac{((-4)^2 - 9)}{(-4 + 3)}$$

$$f(-4) = \frac{(16 - 9)}{(-1)}$$

$$f(-4) = \frac{7}{-1}$$

$$f(-4) = -7$$

## Concepts of Domain and Range

**9. A**

If $g(x)$ is a real number, then $\sqrt{x - 7}$ must be a real number. Therefore, $x - 7$ must be zero or a positive number: $x - 7 \geq 0$, and so $x \geq 7$. Any number less than 7, such as choice (A), is outside the domain of the function.

## Functions as Models

**10. A**

Making inferences from a linear graph can be difficult, but remember that you can write in your test booklet. Use a straight surface or your free hand to extend the line on the graph. By looking at the graph, we can see that each year the tuition of college Y increases. In 2000, tuition was $9,000. So, we know that in 1999 it should be less than that.

## Linear Functions—Equations and Graphs

**11. E**

One question on Test Day might require you to evaluate the graph of a linear function, perhaps by indicating the value of $y$ for a given value of $x$. This question essentially asks you to identify which value of $y$ corresponds to an $x$-value of 0. Locate $x = 0$; then locate the corresponding $y$-value. In this case, that value is 3.

## Quadratic Functions—Equations and Graphs

**12. D**

If you encounter a question about the graph of a quadratic function, it's likely to ask you merely to evaluate a particular point on the graph or, as this question asked, to describe the graph as a whole.

Plug in some points from the graph into each equation to see which ones fit. Good points to test on this graph include (0, 1) and (1, 0):

$$1 = -(0^2) + 1$$
$$0 = -(1^2) + 1$$

Both points work with $y = -x^2 + 1$.

## Geometric Notation for Length, Segments, Lines, Rays, and Congruence

### 13. A

Because the two triangles are congruent, you can combine the information given about each triangle. That is, because $DE = 3$, $CA$ also equals 3. Combining the information from the two triangles gives you:

The height can be found by the Pythagorean theorem, $a^2 + b^2 = c^2$. In this case,

$$3^2 + b^2 = 5^2.$$
$$9 + b^2 = 25$$
$$b^2 = 16$$
$$b = 4$$

The area of the triangle is $\frac{1}{2}(3)(4) = \frac{1}{2}(12) = 6$.

## Trigonometry as an Alternative Method of Solution

### 14. A

If two triangles are congruent, they are identical. Each angle or length in one triangle is equal to the corresponding angle or length in the other triangle. Combine the information in the two triangles to get the following triangle:

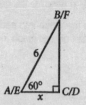

This is a 30-60-90 special triangle, so $x = \frac{1}{2}(6) = 3$.

## Properties of Tangent Lines

**15. C**

When you see a figure that is not drawn to scale, you can often assume that it has been drawn to be deliberately misleading. However, be careful not to assume anything from the apparent positions or lengths of any parts of the figure. Rely instead on the information in the question stem. You may wish to draw your own figure to incorporate that information. This figure includes a circle. Anytime you see a circle, you're going to want its radius at some point. How is the radius of the circle related to the triangle?

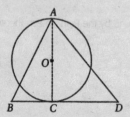

Note: Figure not drawn to scale.

Using the circumference formula and the known circumference of the circle:

$$6\pi = 2\pi r$$

$$r = 3$$

The diagram below has been corrected to include the information in the question stem. Note that because $\overline{BD}$ is tangent to the circle at point C, it is perpendicular to $\overline{OC}$. Because $\overline{AC}$ is a diameter of the circle, it must pass through the center of the circle.

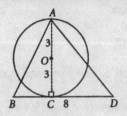

The area of a triangle is one half the length of the base times the height. The height of this triangle is $\overline{AC}$: $3 + 3 = 6$. The area is $\frac{1}{2}(8)(6) = 24$.

## Coordinate Geometry

### 16. C

The distance between two points $(x^1, y^1)$ and $(x^2, y^2)$ can be found by using the distance formula:

$\sqrt{(x_2 - x_1)^2 + (y_2 - y_1)^2}$. Plug in the numbers from the question.
$\sqrt{(7 - 2)^2 + (7 - 4)^2} = \sqrt{5^2 + 3^2} = \sqrt{25 + 9} = \sqrt{34}$

## Qualitative Behavior of Graphs and Functions

### 17. C

Remember, the value of $g(x)$ is the y-value of the graph. Don't worry about how much of the x-axis is shown; it isn't relevant. The largest value of $g(x)$ shown in the figure is 4, at the points $(-5, 4)$ and $(6.5, 4)$.

## Transformations and Their Effect on Graphs of Functions

### 18. C

The graph of $h(x + 1)$ is the graph of $h(x)$ shifted one unit to the left. If you're not sure what that would look like, try comparing a few points from each graph:

$h(3) = h(2 + 1) = 0$
$h(0) = h(-1 + 1) = 3$

## Data Interpretation, Scatterplots, and Matrices

### 19. A

Try to figure out what sort of line would fit these points. What should the slope be? What should the y-intercept be? A line through these points would cross the y-axis at or near 0. Its slope is positive but less than 1. Choice (A) fulfills both these criteria.

## Geometric Probability

### 20. B

There are several different ways to approach this problem, but they all require some knowledge of triangles. Notice that all the triangles in it are 45-45-90 triangles. This allows you to either calculate the ratios between their sides or break them up further, as shown.

Adding two lines to this figure makes it much easier to work with.

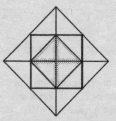

Note that every triangle in this new figure is identical. At this point, you can simply count the number of shaded triangles and divide by the total number of triangles.

$$\frac{4}{16} = \frac{1}{4}.$$

# Chapter Seven: **Math Traps**

- Understanding Order of Difficulty
- Math Trap Test
- Math Trap Diagnostic

## UNDERSTANDING ORDER OF DIFFICULTY

As we've mentioned at least seventeen times, Math sets have usually been arranged in order of difficulty, with the easiest problems coming first and the hardest problems coming last. Knowing this leads you, the test taker, to treat question #3 differently than question #14. This is where SAT Math traps come into play.

If you arrive at an answer choice to a hard Math problem without too much effort, be suspicious; that answer is probably a math trap. Learning how to recognize and avoid common SAT Math traps will help you be more successful on the math sections. There are 10 common Math traps on the SAT. We'll show you the trap, the wrong answer the trap wants you to choose, how to avoid that answer, and how to solve the problem quickly and correctly.

## MATH TRAP TEST

The following ten questions have one thing in common—they all have traps. Take 12 minutes to try to work through all of them. Then check your answers on page 162.

1. Sammy purchased a new Hummer in 2000. Three years later, he sold it to a dealer for 40 percent less than he paid for it in 2000. The dealer then added 20 percent onto the price he paid and resold it to another customer. The price the final customer paid for the Hummer was what percent of the original price Sammy paid in 2000?

   (A) 40%
   (B) 60%
   (C) 72%
   (D) 80%
   (E) 88%

2. In a class of 27 plumbers, the average (arithmetic mean) score of the male plumbers on the final exam was 83. If the average score of the 15 female plumbers in the class was 92, what was the average of the whole class?

   (A) 86.2
   (B) 87.0
   (C) 87.5
   (D) 88.0
   (E) 88.2

3. Mammo's coin collection consists of quarters, dimes, and nickels. If the ratio of the number of quarters to the number of dimes is 5:2, and the ratio of the number of dimes to the number of nickels is 3:4, what is the ratio of the number of quarters to the number of nickels?

   (A)  5:4
   (B)  7:5
   (C)  10:6
   (D)  12:7
   (E)  15:8

4. What is the least positive integer that is divisible by both 2 and 5 and leaves a remainder of 3 when divided by 11?

   (A)  30
   (B)  32
   (C)  33
   (D)  70
   (E)  80

5. What number is $33\frac{1}{3}$% less than 9?

6. The ratio of two quantities is 3:4. If each of the quantities is increased by 1, what is the ratio of these two new quantities?

(A) $\dfrac{9}{16}$

(B) $\dfrac{2}{3}$

(C) $\dfrac{3}{4}$

(D) $\dfrac{4}{5}$

(E) It cannot be determined from the information given.

7. If $n \neq 0$, then which of the following must be true?

I. $n^2 > n$

II. $2n > n$

III. $n + 1 > n$

(A) I only

(B) II only

(C) III only

(D) I and III only

(E) I, II, and III

8. At a certain restaurant, the hourly wage for a waiter is 20 percent more than the hourly wage for a dishwasher, and the hourly wage for a dishwasher is half as much as the hourly wage for a cook's assistant. If a cook's assistant earns $8.50 per hour, how much less than a cook's assistant does a waiter earn each hour?

   (A) $2.55
   (B) $3.40
   (C) $4.25
   (D) $5.10
   (E) $5.95

9. A car traveled from A to B at an average speed of 40 mph and then immediately traveled back from B to A at an average speed of 60 mph. What was the car's average speed for the roundtrip in miles per hour?

   (A) 45
   (B) 48
   (C) 50
   (D) 52
   (E) 54

10. The tickets for a certain raffle are consecutively numbered. If Louis sold the tickets numbered from 75 to 148 inclusive, how many raffle tickets did he sell?

    (A) 71
    (B) 72
    (C) 73
    (D) 74
    (E) 75

## How Did You Do?

Here are the answers:

1. (C), 2. (D), 3. (E), 4. (E), 5. (6), 6. (E), 7. (C), 8. (B), 9. (B), 10. (D)

Unless you calculated incorrectly, chances are your incorrect answers are an indication that you got caught in a trap. The same traps occur again and again on the SAT. If you learn how they work and how to avoid them, dealing with even the hardest traps will become easy, and you'll do much better on the harder math questions. To see how they work, let's take another look at the 10 sample questions. Each contains one of the Top 10 Math Traps.

## TRAP 1: PERCENT INCREASE/DECREASE

Sammy purchased a new Hummer in 2000. Three years later, he sold it to a dealer for 40 percent less than he paid for it in 2000. The dealer then added 20 percent onto the price he paid and resold it to another customer. The price the final customer paid for the Hummer was what percent of the original price Sammy paid in 2000?

(A) 40%

(B) 60%

(C) 72%

(D) 80%

(E) 88%

## The Wrong Answer

The increase/decrease percentage problem usually appears at the end of a section and invariably contains a trap. Most students will figure that taking away 40 percent and then adding 20 percent will give them an overall loss of 20 percent, and they'll pick choice (D), 80 percent, as the correct answer. Those students would be wrong.

## The Trap

When a quantity is increased or decreased by a percentage more than once, you can't simply add and subtract the percentages to get the answer. In this kind of percentage problem, the first change is a percentage of the starting amount, but the second change is a percentage of the new amount.

## Avoiding the Trap

Don't blindly add and subtract percentages. They can be added and subtracted only when they are of the same amount.

## Finding the Right Answer

We know:

- The *40 percent less* that Sammy got for the Hummer is 40 percent of his original price.
- The 20 percent the dealer adds on is 20 percent of what the dealer paid, which is a much smaller amount.
- Adding 20 percent of that smaller amount is *not* the same thing as adding back 20 percent of the original price.

## Solving the Problem Fast

Use 100 for a starting quantity, even it's not plausible in the real situation. The problem asks for the relative amount of change. So you can take any starting number and compare it with the final result. Because you're dealing with percentages, 100 is the easiest number to work with.

- If Sammy paid $100 for the Hummer, what is 40 percent less?
- In the case of $100, each percent equals $1, so $100 - 40 = 60$. Sammy sold the Hummer for $60.
- If the dealer charges 20 percent more than his purchase price, she's raising the price by 20 percent of $60, which is $60 \times 0.20 = \$12$ (not 20 percent of $100, which would be $20!).
- Therefore, the dealer sold the Hummer again for $60 + $12, or $72.
- Finally, what percent of the starting price ($100) is $72? It's 72%. So the correct answer here is choice (C).

## TRAP 2: WEIGHTED AVERAGES

In a class of 27 plumbers, the average (arithmetic mean) score of the male plumbers on the final exam was 83. If the average score of the 15 female plumbers in the class was 92, what was the average of the whole class?

(A) 86.2

(B) 87.0

(C) 87.5

(D) 88.0

(E) 88.2

### The Wrong Answer

Some students will rush in and simply average 83 and 92 to come up with 87.5 as the class average. Those students will be wrong.

### The Trap

You cannot combine averages of different quantities by taking the average of those original averages. In an averages problem, if one value occurs more frequently than others, it is *weighted* more. Remember, the average formula calls for the sum of all the terms divided by the total number of terms.

### Avoiding the Trap

Don't just take the average of the averages; work with the sums.

### Finding the Right Answer

If 15 of the 27 plumbers are female, the remaining 12 must be male. We can't just add 83 to 92 and divide by two. In this class, there are more females than males, and therefore, the females' test scores are *weighted* more—they contribute more to the class average. So the answer must be either (D) or (E).

To find each sum, multiply each average by the number of terms it represents. After you have found the sums of the different terms, find the combined average by plugging them into the average formula.

$$\text{Total class average} = \frac{\text{Sum of females' scores} + \text{Sum of males' scores}}{\text{Total number of students}}$$

$$= \frac{(\# \text{ of females} \times \text{females' average score}) + (\# \text{ of males} \times \text{males' average score})}{\text{Total number of students}}$$

$$= \frac{15(92) + 12(83)}{27} = \frac{1,380 + 996}{27} = 88$$

So the class average is 88, answer choice (D).

## TRAP 3: RATIO:RATIO:RATIO

Mammo's coin collection consists of quarters, dimes, and nickels. If the ratio of the number of quarters to the number of dimes is 5:2, and the ratio of the number of dimes to the number of nickels is 3:4, what is the ratio of the number of quarters to the number of nickels?

(A)  5:4

(B)  7:5

(C)  10:6

(D)  12:7

(E)  15:8

## The Wrong Answer

If you chose 5:4 as the correct answer, you fell for the classic ratio trap.

## The Trap

Parts of different ratios don't always refer to the same whole. In the classic ratio trap, two different ratios each share a common part that is represented by two different numbers. However, the two ratios do not refer to the same whole, so they are not in proportion to each other.

To solve this type of problem, restate both ratios so the numbers representing the common part (in this case *dimes*) are the same. Then all the parts will be in proportion and can be compared to each other.

## Avoiding the Trap

Restate ratios so the same number refers to the same quantity. Make sure the common quantity in both ratios has the same number.

## Finding the Right Answer

To find the ratio of quarters to nickels, restate both ratios so that the number of dimes is the same in both. You are given two ratios:

quarters to dimes = 5:2      dimes to nickels = 3:4

- The number corresponding to dimes in the first ratio is 2.
- The number corresponding to dimes in the second ratio is 3.
- To restate the ratios, find the least common multiple of 2 and 3.
- The least common multiple of 2 and 3 is 2 × 3, or 6.

Restate the ratios with the number of dimes as 6:

quarters to dimes = 15:6 (which is the same as 5:2)

dimes to nickels = 6:8 (which is the same as 3:4)

The ratios are still in their original proportions, but now they can be compared easily because dimes are represented by the same number in both. The ratio of quarters to dimes to nickels is 15:6:8, so the ratio of quarters to nickels is 15:8, which is answer choice (E).

## TRAP 4: "LEAST" AND "GREATEST"

What is the least positive integer that is divisible by both 2 and 5 and leaves a remainder of 3 when divided by 11?

(A) 30

(B) 32

(C) 33

(D) 70

(E) 80

### The Wrong Answer

(A) is the choice *not* to go for here.

### The Trap

In questions that ask for the *least, minimum, or smallest* something, the choice offering the smallest number is rarely right. In questions that ask for the *greatest, maximum, or largest* something, the choice offering the largest number is very rarely right.

### Avoiding the Trap

Consider the constraints and requirements that the nature of the question has placed upon the possible answer. Don't leap to conclusions. In fact, if you ever need to guess on questions asking about the least number, the one place *not* to go is to the smallest choice and *vice versa* for questions asking about the largest number.

### Finding the Right Answer

If the integer is divisible by both 2 and 5, it is a multiple of 2, 5, or 10, so eliminate (B) and (C). If it leaves a remainder of 3 when divided by 11, it is 3 more than a multiple of 11. In (A), $33 - 3 = 27$, which isn't a multiple of 11. In (D), $77 - 3 = 67$, which isn't a multiple of 11. In (E), $80 - 3 = 77$, which is a multiple of 11, and the correct answer.

## TRAP 5: PERCENT "OF" VERSUS PERCENT "LESS" OR "GREATER"

### What number is $33\frac{1}{3}$ % less than 9?

**The Wrong Answer**

Three.

**The Trap**

Reading too quickly or with insufficient care could lead a test taker to mistake $33\frac{1}{3}$% less than 9 for $33\frac{1}{3}$% of 9, which is $\frac{1}{3} \times 9 = 3$.

**Avoiding the Trap**

Be on the lookout for subtleties of wording, especially in questions appearing in the middle or end of a section. Consciously and actively distinguish these three things whenever percent questions arise:

*a* percent *of b*;

*a* percent *less than b*;

*a* percent *greater than b*.

For example:

25 percent *of* 8 means .25(8);

25 percent *less than* 8 means 8 − (.25)(8);

25 percent *greater than* 8 means 8 + (.25)(8).

**Finding the Right Answer**

$33\frac{1}{3}$% less than 9 means $9 - \left(\frac{1}{3}\right)(9) = 9 - 3 = 6$.

## TRAP 6: RATIO VERSUS QUANTITY

The ratio of two quantities is 3:4. If each of the quantities is increased by 1, what is the ratio of these two new quantities?

(A) $\dfrac{9}{16}$

(B) $\dfrac{2}{3}$

(C) $\dfrac{3}{4}$

(D) $\dfrac{4}{5}$

(E) It cannot be determined from the information given.

### The Wrong Answer

(D) is a trap.

### The Trap

If all you have is a ratio, you cannot simply add to or subtract from the parts at will. Test takers unfamiliar with this rule would probably add 1 to 3 and to 4, coming up incorrectly with the ratio of 4:5.

### Avoiding the Trap

Avoid this trap by remembering the rule that you can multiply or divide a ratio or part of a ratio, but you cannot add to or subtract from a ratio or part of a ratio. Consider some examples. Imagine that at a meeting, the ratio of women to men is 6:5. If the number of women doubles, the new ratio of women to men is 12:5. In other words, you can multiply a ratio or part of a ratio. Similarly, you can divide a ratio or part of a ratio. Given the original ratio of women to men as 6:5, you can conclude that if the number of women at the meeting were cut in half, the new ratio of women to men at the meeting would be 3:5.

However, you cannot add to or subtract from a ratio or part of a ratio because knowing the ratio doesn't tell you the actual quantities associated with it. To clearly understand what we mean, we will explain two scenarios. Again considering a meeting at which the ratio of women to men is 6:5, assume that in situation I, the actual quantities of women and men are 12 and 10, respectively. Assume that in situation II the actual quantities of women and men are 18 and 15, respectively. Now assume that one woman and one man enter the meeting. In situation I, the new ratio of women to men is 13:11. In situation II, the new ratio of women to men is 19:16. It is obvious in this example that $\frac{13}{11} \neq \frac{19}{16}$; thus, this inequality demonstrates how it is possible to have the same ratio and get different results depending on the quantities with which you begin.

## Finding the Right Answer

For students on the lookout for violations of the rule we've been discussing, this question means quick points. Once you realize that the ratio of the new quantities depends on the actual original quantities—not simply their ratio—you'll quickly recognize that the answer cannot be determined from the information provided. The correct answer is (E).

## TRAP 7: NOT ALL NUMBERS ARE POSITIVE INTEGERS

If $n \neq 0$, then which of the following must be
true?

I. $n^2 > n$

II. $2n > n$

III. $n + 1 > n$

(A) I only

(B) II only

(C) III only

(D) I and III only

(E) I, II, and III

### The Wrong Answer

In the example above, if you considered only positive integers greater
than 1 for the value of $n$, you would assume that all three statements
are true. However, that is not the case.

### The Trap

Not all numbers are positive integers. Don't forget there are negative
numbers and fractions as well. This is important because negative
numbers and fractions between 0 and 1 behave very differently from
positive integers.

### Avoiding the Trap

When picking numbers for variables, consider fractions and negative
numbers.

## Finding the Right Answer

Looking at statement I, you can assume that squaring a number will give a larger number as a result. For example, $4^2 = 16$, or $10^2 = 100$. However, when you square a fraction between 0 and 1, the result is quite different. $\left(\frac{1}{2}\right)^2 = \frac{1}{4}$; $\left(\frac{1}{10}\right)^2 = \frac{1}{100}$. So, when you square a fraction, the resulting fraction will be a smaller number.

In statement II, what happens when you multiply a number by 2? $7 \times 2 = 14$; $25 \times 2 = 50$. Multiplying any positive number by 2 doubles that number, so you get a larger result. However, if you multiply a negative number by 2, your result is smaller than the original number. For example, $-3 \times 2 = -6$.

Finally, look at statement III. What happens when you add 1 to any number? Adding 1 to any number gives you a larger number as a result. For example, $5 + 1 = 6$; $\frac{1}{2} + 1 = 1\frac{1}{2}$; and $-7 + 1 = -6$.

Therefore, only statement III must be true, so choice (C) is correct. If you didn't consider fractions or negative numbers, you would have fallen into the trap and answered the question incorrectly.

## TRAP 8: HIDDEN INSTRUCTIONS

At a certain restaurant, the hourly wage for a
waiter is 20 percent more than the hourly wage
for a dishwasher, and the hourly wage for a
dishwasher is half as much as the hourly wage
for a cook's assistant. If a cook's assistant earns
$8.50 per hour, how much less than a cook's
assistant does a waiter earn each hour?

(A)  $2.55

(B)  $3.40

(C)  $4.25

(D)  $5.10

(E)  $5.95

### The Wrong Answer

To solve this problem, you must find the hourly wage of the waiter.
The cook's assistant earns $8.50 per hour. The dishwasher earns half
of this—$4.25 per hour. The waiter earns 20 percent more than the
dishwasher—$4.25 × 1.2 = $5.10. So the waiter earns $5.10 per
hour, and your automatic reaction might be to fill in answer choice
(D). But (D) is the wrong answer.

### The Trap

A small clue, easily overlooked, can mean the difference between a
right and wrong answer. In this case, the word is *less* is that small
clue. After spending all this time finding the waiter's hourly wage, in
their moment of triumph, many students skip right over the vital last
step. They overlook that the question asks not what the waiter earns,
but how much less than the cook's assistant the waiter earns.

## Avoiding the Trap

Make sure you answer the question that's being asked. Watch out for hidden instructions.

## Finding the Right Answer

You have figured out that the waiter earns $5.10 per hour, and the cook's assistant earns $8.50 per hour. To find out how much less the waiter earns than the cook's assistant, subtract the waiter's hourly wage from the cook's assistant's hourly wage. The correct answer is (B).

## TRAP 9: AVERAGE RATES

A car traveled from $A$ to $B$ at an average speed of 40 mph and then immediately traveled back from $B$ to $A$ at an average speed of 60 mph. What was the car's average speed for the roundtrip in miles per hour?

(A) 45

(B) 48

(C) 50

(D) 52

(E) 54

## The Wrong Answer

Do you see which answer choice looks too good to be true? The temptation is simply to add 40 and 60 and divide by two. The answer is *obviously* 50 (C). But 50 is wrong.

## The Trap

To get an average speed, you can't just average the rates. Why is the average speed not 50 mph? Because the car spent more time traveling at 40 mph than at 60 mph. Each leg of the round trip was the same distance, but the first leg, at the slower speed, took more time.

## Avoiding the Trap

You can solve almost any Average Rate problem with this general formula:

$$\text{Average Rate} = \frac{\text{Total distance}}{\text{Total times}}$$

Use the given information to figure out the total distance and the total time. But how can you do that when many problems don't specify the distances?

## Finding the Right Answer

In our sample above, we are told that a car went from $A$ to $B$ at 40 mph and back from $B$ to $A$ at 60 mph. In other words, it went half the total distance at 40 mph and half the total distance at 60 mph.

How do you use the formula:

$$\text{Average Rate} = \frac{\text{Total distance}}{\text{Total times}}?$$

If the total distance is not provided, pick a number! Pick any number you want for the total distance. Divide that total distance into half distances. Calculate the time needed to travel each half distance at the different rates.

Make sure to pick a number that's easy to work with. A good number to pick here would be 240 miles for the total distance because you can figure in your head the times for two 120-mile legs at 40 mph and 60 mph:

$$A \text{ to } B: = \frac{120 \text{ miles}}{40 \text{ miles per hour}} = 3 \text{ hours}$$

$$B \text{ to } A: = \frac{120 \text{ miles}}{60 \text{ miles per hour}} = 2 \text{ hours}$$

Total time = 5 hours

Now plug "total distance = 240 miles" and "total time = 5 hours" into the general formula:

Average Rate = $\frac{\text{Total distance}}{\text{Total times}}$ = $\frac{240 \text{ miles}}{5 \text{ hours}}$ = 48 miles per hour

Correct answer: (B).

## TRAP 10: COUNTING NUMBERS

The tickets for a certain raffle are consecutively numbered. If Louis sold the tickets numbered from 75 to 148 inclusive, how many raffle tickets did he sell?

(A) 71

(B) 72

(C) 73

(D) 74

(E) 75

### The Wrong Answer

If you subtract 75 from 148 and get 73 as the answer, you are wrong.

### The Trap

Subtracting the first and last integers in a range will give you the difference of the two numbers. It won't give you the number of integers in that range.

### Avoiding the Trap

To count the number of integers in a range, subtract and then add 1. If you forget the rule, pick two small numbers that are close together, such as 1 and 4. Obviously, there are four integers from 1 to 4, inclusive. But if you had subtracted 1 from 4, your remainder would have been 3.

## Finding the Right Answer

In the problem above, subtract 75 from 148. The result is 73. Add 1 to this difference to get the number of integers. That gives you 74. The correct answer is (D). The word *inclusive* tells you to include the first and last numbers given. So, for example, the integers from 5 to 15 inclusive would include 5 and 15. Questions always make it clear whether you should include the outer numbers or not because the correct answer hinges on this point.

## PRACTICE

**Directions:** Identify the trap in each problem (and solve the problem correctly). Answers are found on page 182. There's no time limit.

1. If $x$ is 300 percent of 25 and $y$ is 25 percent more than 40, then $x$ is what percent of $y$? (Disregard the % sign when you grid your answer.)

2. In the figure above, what is the maximum number of nonoverlapping regions into which the shaded area can be divided using exactly two straight lines?

(A) 3

(B) 4

(C) 5

(D) 6

(E) 7

3. A certain school event was open only to juniors and seniors. Half the number of juniors who had planned to attend actually attended. Double the number of seniors who had planned to attend actually attended. If the ratio of the number of juniors who had planned to attend to the number of seniors who had planned to attend was 4 to 5, then juniors were what fraction of attendees?

(A) $\frac{1}{6}$

(B) $\frac{1}{5}$

(C) $\frac{4}{19}$

(D) $\frac{4}{15}$

(E) It cannot be determined from the information given.

4. If $p - q = 4$ and $r$ is the number of integers less than $p$ and greater than $q$, then which of the following could be true?

   I.  $r = 3$

  II.  $r = 4$

 III.  $r = 5$

(A) I only

(B) II only

(C) III only

(D) I and II

(E) I, II, and III

5. Pump #1 can drain a 400-gallon water tank in 1.2 hours. Pump #2 can drain the same tank in 1.8 hours. How many minutes longer than pump #1 would it take pump #2 to drain a 100-gallon tank?

(A) 0.15

(B) 1.2

(C) 6

(D) 9

(E) 18

6. Volumes 12 through 30 of a certain encyclopedia are located on the bottom shelf of a bookcase. If the volumes of the encyclopedia are numbered consecutively, how many volumes of the encyclopedia are on the bottom shelf?

(A) 17

(B) 18

(C) 19

(D) 29

(E) 30

7. A reservoir is at full capacity at the beginning of summer. By the first day of fall, the level in the reservoir is 30 percent below full capacity. Then during the fall, a period of heavy rains increases the level by 30 percent. After the rains, the reservoir is at what percent of its full capacity?

   (A)  60%
   (B)  85%
   (C)  91%
   (D)  95%
   (E)  100%

8. Two classes, one with 50 students and the other with 30, take the same exam. The combined average of both classes is 84.5. If the larger class averages 80, what is the average of the smaller class?

   (A)  87.2
   (B)  89.0
   (C)  92.0
   (D)  93.3
   (E)  94.5

9. In a pet shop, the ratio of puppies to kittens is 7:6, and the ratio of kittens to guinea pigs is 5:3. What is the ratio of puppies to guinea pigs?

   (A)  7:3
   (B)  6:5
   (C)  13:8
   (D)  21:11
   (E)  35:18

10. A typist typed the first $n$ pages of a book,
    where $n > 0$, at an average rate of 12 pages per
    hour and typed the remaining $n$ pages at an
    average rate of 20 pages per hour. What was
    the typist's average rate in pages per hour for
    the entire book?

    (A) 14
    (B) 15
    (C) 16
    (D) 17
    (E) 18

## REMEMBER...

The SAT loves to use traps on harder math problems. Their favorite
ten traps are:

Trap 1: Percent Increase/Decrease

Trap 2: Weighted Averages

Trap 3: Ratio:Ratio:Ratio

Trap 4: "Least" and "Greatest"

Trap 5: Percent "Of" Versus Percent "Less" or "Greater"

Trap 6: Ratio Versus Quantity

Trap 7: Not All Numbers Are Positive Integers

Trap 8: Hidden Instructions

Trap 9: Average Rates

Trap 10: Counting Numbers

## ANSWERS: DID YOU FALL FOR THE TRAPS?

Each wrong answer represents one trap you need to work on. Go back and reread the section on that trap. Then look at the practice set's problem again. Do you see the trap now?

1.  150 (Trap 5)
2.  C (Trap 4)
3.  A (Trap 6)
4.  D (Trap 7)
5.  D (Trap 8)
6.  C (Trap 10)
7.  C (Trap 1)
8.  C (Trap 2)
9.  E (Trap 3)
10. B (Trap 9)

# Chapter Eight: **Strategies for SAT Reading Comprehension Questions**

- **Strategies for Short Passages**
- **Extra Strategies for Long Passages**
- **Tactics for Paired Passages**

The Critical Reading section of the SAT has two kinds of questions: Reading Comprehension questions and Sentence Completion questions. We're going to give you our best strategies for attacking both of these question types in the next two chapters. We'll start now with Reading Comprehension, because most students consider it the "hardest" part of the Critical Reading section, and the SAT has tried to make it even harder in 2005.

In 2005, for the first time ever, the SAT has divided its Reading Comprehension questions into two types—short passages and long passages. The SAT has always used long passages (several paragraphs totaling 400 to 850 words). The short passages are the new kids on the block. They are single paragraphs of about 100–150 words.

The two types of passages are more alike than different, and they are predictable, since the test makers use a formula to write them. The topics are drawn from the arts, humanities, social sciences, natural sciences, and fiction.

The questions are also predictable. You'll be asked about the overall tone and content of a paragraph, the details, and what the author suggests. You may also have a few "paired paragraph" question sets consisting of two related excerpts with questions that ask you to compare and contrast the related paragraphs. Here are some general strategies.

## DON'T GET BOGGED DOWN

Reading Comprehension questions are NOT ordered by difficulty. Unlike Sentence Completion questions (covered in chapter 9), the location of a Reading Comprehension question tells you nothing about its difficulty. So don't get bogged down on a hard Reading Comprehension question. The next one might be a lot easier for you, and both questions are worth the same amount of points.

## SHORT PASSAGES FIRST

You should answer all of the questions for short passages before attacking the longer passages. Again, every question is worth the same number of points, so answer the ones you find easier before moving on to the tough stuff.

## KNOW THE DIRECTIONS

The instructions for the Critical Reading section are short and sweet:

Answer the questions based on the information in the accompanying passage or passages.

Here's the best way to do that.

## HOW TO READ A PASSAGE

Each Reading Comprehension passage is written for a purpose: The author wants to make a point, describe a situation, or convince you of his or her ideas. (The SAT test makers want to see if you can identify meanings, make inferences, and spot themes.)

## Seriously Skim

As you're reading, ask yourself:

- What's this passage about?
- What's the point of this?
- Why did someone write this?
- What's the author trying to say?
- What are the two or three most important things in this passage?

This is active reading, and it's the key to staying focused on the page. Active reading does *not* mean reading the passage word-for-word. It means reading lightly, but with a focus—in other words, *serious skimming*. The questions themselves help you fill in the details by directing you back to important information in the passage.

Getting hung up on details is a major Reading Comprehension pitfall. You need to grasp the outline, but you don't need to get all the fine features. Most questions hinge on understanding the author's point of view, not recalling obscure details buried somewhere in the passage.

### HOW TO SERIOUSLY SKIM

Skim the passage to get the writer's drift. Don't read the passage thoroughly. It's a waste of time.

As you skim, search for important points. Don't wait for important information to jump out and hit you in the face.

Don't get caught up in details. The questions will often supply them for you, or tell you exactly how to find them.

## Serious Skimming Practice

Test your reading skills on the following short passages, keeping our Serious Skimming tips in mind. Serious skimming should make these challenging passages—and every passage—more manageable.

### Paragraph A

Recently, at my grandmother's eightieth birthday party, my family looked at old photographs.

In one of them I see a scared little boy holding tightly to his mother's skirt, and I scarcely recognize myself. My foremost memory of that time is simply being cold—the mild Vietnamese winters that I had known couldn't prepare me for the bitter winds of the American Midwest. The cold seemed emblematic of everything I hated about my new country—we had no friends, no extended family, and we all lived together in a two-room apartment. My mother, ever shrewd, remarked that selling heat in such a cold place would surely bring fortune, and she was right. My parents now own a successful heating supply company.

### Paragraph B

Many mammals instinctively raise their fur when they are cold—a reaction effected by tiny muscles just under the skin which surround hair follicles. When the muscles contract, the hairs stand up, creating an increased air space under the fur. The air space provides more effective insulation for the mammal's body, thus allowing it to retain more heat for longer periods of time. Some animals also raise their fur when they are challenged by predators or even other members of their own species. The raised fur makes the animal appear slightly bigger, and, ideally, more powerful. Interestingly, though devoid of fur, humans still retain this instinct. So, the next time a horror movie gives you "goosebumps," remember that your skin is following a deep-seated mammalian impulse now rendered obsolete.

**Paragraph C**

Elizabeth Barrett Browning, a feminist writer of the Victorian Era, used her poetry and prose to take on a wide range of issues facing her society, including "the woman question." In her long poem "Aurora Leigh," she explores this question as she portrays both the growth of the artist and the growth of the woman within. Aurora Leigh is not a traditional Victorian woman—she is well educated and self-sufficient. In the poem, Browning argues that the limitations placed on women in contrast to the freedom men enjoy should incite women to rise up and effect a change in their circumstances. Browning's writing, including "Aurora Leigh," helped to pave the way for major social change in women's lives.

## KAPLAN'S READING COMPREHENSION ATTACK STRATEGY

Serious skimming is a vital component of Kaplan's method for attacking Reading Comprehension questions. Once you have seriously skimmed the passage, here's how you attack the questions:

1. Read the question stem.
2. Locate the material you need.
3. Predict the answer.
4. Scan the answer choices.
5. Select your answer.

### 1. Read the Question Stem

This is the place to really read carefully. Take a second to make sure you understand what the question is asking.

## 2. Locate the Material You Need

If you are given a line reference, read the material surrounding the line mentioned. It will clarify exactly what the question is asking. If you're not given a line reference, scan the text to find the place where the question applies, and quickly reread those few sentences. Keep the main point of the passage in mind.

## 3. Predict the Answer

Don't spend time making up a precise answer. You need only a general sense of what you're after, so you can recognize the correct answer quickly when you read the choices.

## 4. Scan the Answer Choices

Scan the choices, looking for one that fits your idea of the right answer. If you don't find an ideal answer, quickly eliminate wrong choices by checking back to the passage. Rule out choices that are too extreme or go against common sense. Get rid of answers that sound reasonable, but don't make sense in the context of the passage. Don't pick farfetched inferences. SAT inferences tend to be strongly implied in the passage.

## 5. Select Your Answer

You've eliminated the obvious wrong answers. One of the remaining should fit your ideal. If you're left with more than one contender, consider the passage's main idea, and make your best guess.

### Practice Kaplan's Attack Strategy

Try Kaplan's attack strategy on the passage and question that follow.

### Question 1 is based on the following short passage.

Recently, at my grandmother's eightieth birthday party, my family looked at old photographs.
In one of them I see a scared little boy holding
tightly to his mother's skirt, and I scarcely recog-
5 nize myself. My foremost memory of that time is

simply being cold—the mild Vietnamese winters
that I had known couldn't prepare me for the
bitter winds of the American Midwest. The cold
seemed emblematic of everything I hated about
10  my new country—we had no friends, no extended family, and we all lived together in a two-
room apartment. My mother, ever shrewd,
remarked that selling heat in such a cold place
would surely bring fortune, and she was right.
15  My parents now own a successful heating supply
company.

   1. The author's attitude toward the "scared little
      boy" mentioned in line 3, indicates that the
      author

     (A)  is unsure that the photograph is actually
          of his family

     (B)  believes that the boy is likely overly
          dependent on his mother

     (C)  feels that he has himself changed consid-
          erably since childhood

     (D)  regards his mother's strategy to sell heat-
          ing supplies as clever

     (E)  regrets his family's move to the United
          States

## 1. Read the Question Stem

In this case, the question is straightforward: What does the author
think about the little boy?

## 2. Locate the Material You Need

You're given line reference, so be sure and go back to that line. But
don't read just that specific line—read a line or two before and after
as well. When you do, you see that the author says that he scarcely

recognizes himself. From this, you know that the author is looking at a picture of himself as a boy.

### 3. Predict the Answer

Why would the author say that he scarcely recognizes himself? Surely it's not meant literally—he does recognize himself, but it's hard for him to believe he's so different now. (You may have had a similar feeling when looking at a picture of yourself as a little kid.) So, look for an answer choice that matches this prediction.

### 4. Scan the Answer Choices

(A) is too literal—the author is speaking figuratively when he says he scarcely recognizes the boy.

(B) goes too far in making an inference. Although the boy is sticking close to his mom in the picture, that doesn't mean that the author thinks this is a bad thing.

(C) is a great match for your prediction, and is the correct answer.

(D) might be a true statement, but it comes from later in the passage. It has nothing to do with the author's attitude toward the boy in the picture.

(E), like (B), is too great a leap, and can't safely be inferred from the info in the passage.

### 5. Select Your Answer

(C) was right in line with your prediction, but if you didn't spot it or weren't sure, you could still get the question right by eliminating the wrong answers.

## SHORT PASSAGE PRACTICE

Now try Kaplan's Attack Strategy on the remaining questions for these short passages. Answers are on page 215.

**Question 2 is based on the following passage.**

Recently, at my grandmother's eightieth birthday party, my family looked at old photographs.
In one of them I see a scared little boy holding
tightly to his mother's skirt, and I scarcely recog-
5 nize myself. My foremost memory of that time is
simply being cold—the mild Vietnamese winters
that I had known couldn't prepare me for the
bitter winds of the American Midwest. The cold
seemed emblematic of everything I hated about
10 my new country—we had no friends, no extended family, and we all lived together in a two-
room apartment. My mother, ever shrewd,
remarked that selling heat in such a cold place
would surely bring fortune, and she was right.
15 My parents now own a successful heating supply
company.

2. Lines 12–14 suggest that the author's mother
   regarded the cold of the American Midwest as

   (A) more drastic than that of Vietnam

   (B) an opportunity for economic success

   (C) an obstacle to familial happiness

   (D) symbolic of other challenges and
       problems

   (E) unimportant to the family's future

**Questions 3–4 are based on the following passage.**

Many mammals instinctively raise their fur
when they are cold—a reaction effected by tiny
muscles just under the skin which surround hair
follicles. When the muscles contract, the hairs
5 stand up, creating an increased air space under
the fur. The air space provides more effective
insulation for the mammal's body, thus allowing
it to retain more heat for longer periods of time.
Some animals also raise their fur when they are
10 challenged by predators or even other members
of their own species. The raised fur makes the
animal appear slightly bigger, and, ideally, more
powerful. Interestingly, though devoid of fur,
humans still retain this instinct. So, the next time
15 a horror movie gives you "goosebumps," remember that your skin is following a deep-seated
mammalian impulse now rendered obsolete.

3. The "increased air space under the fur" mentioned in lines 5–6 serves primarily to

   (A) combat cold

   (B) intimidate other animals

   (C) render such measures obsolete

   (D) cool over-heated predators

   (E) make mammals more powerful

4. Based on the passage, the author would most
   likely describe "goosebumps" in humans as

   (A) an unnecessary and unexplained
        phenomenon

   (B) a harmful but necessary measure

   (C) an amusing but dangerous feature

   (D) an interesting evolutionary remnant

   (E) a powerful but infrequent occurrence

**Questions 5–6 are based on the following passage.**

Elizabeth Barrett Browning, a feminist writer
of the Victorian Era, used her poetry and prose to
take on a wide range of issues facing her society,
including "the woman question." In her long
5  poem "Aurora Leigh," she explores this question
as she portrays both the growth of the artist and
the growth of the woman within. Aurora Leigh is
not a traditional Victorian woman—she is well
educated and self-sufficient. In the poem,
10  Browning argues that the limitations placed on
women in contrast to the freedom men enjoy
should incite women to rise up and effect a
change in their circumstances. Browning's writing, including "Aurora Leigh," helped to pave the
15  way for major social change in women's lives.

5. It can be inferred from the passage that the
   author believes that the traditional Victorian
   woman

   (A)  wrote poetry

   (B)  was portrayed accurately in
        "Aurora Leigh"

   (C)  fought for social change

   (D)  was not well educated

   (E)  had a public role in society

6. As used in line 12, "effect" most nearly means

   (A)  imitate

   (B)  result

   (C)  cause

   (D)  disturb

   (E)  prevent

## THE SAT'S FAVORITE READING COMPREHENSION QUESTIONS

We have covered how to read the passages and how to attack the questions. Now we're going to tip you off on the kinds of Reading Comprehension questions the SAT writes over and over again.

Most Reading Comprehension questions fall into three basic types. "Big Picture" questions test your overall understanding of the passage's biggest points. "Little Picture" questions ask about localized bits of information. About 70 percent of Critical Reading questions are "Little Picture." Vocabulary-in-Context questions ask for the meaning of a single word.

In the preceding questions, question 4 was an example of a Big Picture question. Question 3 was an example of a Little Picture question. Question 6 was a Vocabulary-in-Context question.

### Big Picture Questions

Big Picture questions test your overall understanding of a passage. They ask about:

- The main point or purpose of a passage
- The author's attitude or tone
- The logic underlying the author's argument
- How ideas relate to each other

The best way to find a passage's Big Picture is to read actively. As you read, ask yourself, "What's this all about? What's the point of this?" Let's return to question four. It's a Big Picture question, asking for the author's attitude toward the subject of the passage. Use our five-step attack strategy to find your answer:

> Based on the passage, the author would most likely describe "goosebumps" in humans as
>
> (A) an unnecessary and unexplained phenomenon
>
> (B) a harmful but necessary measure
>
> (C) an amusing but dangerous feature
>
> (D) a useless but interesting remnant
>
> (E) a powerful but infrequent occurrence

## 1. Read the Question Stem
Simple enough: What does the author think about goosebumps?

## 2. Locate the Material You Need
In this case, you're asked about the overall point, so you probably don't need to go back to a specific part of the passage. Instead, quickly summarize the author's point, as though you wanted to explain it to a younger brother or sister. (You want to boil everything down to the simplest possible terms.)

## 3. Predict the Answer
You might say something like, "Goosebumps are left over from when people had fur."

## 4. Scan the Answer Choices
(A)—*unnecessary* fits, but *unexplained* is wrong. (The whole passage was written to explain goosebumps.)

(B)—goosebumps seem to do no harm, and don't seem to be necessary in people, so this one's doubly wrong.

(C)—*amusing* maybe, but *dangerous* doesn't fit.

(D)—that looks very good. (The author must think it's pretty interesting, or she wouldn't have written the passage in the first place.)

(E)—the passage never talks about the frequency, and *powerful* doesn't really fit.

## 5. Select Your Answer
Only (D) fits, so that's your answer.

Here's a great tip: If you're still stumped on a Big Picture question after reading the passage, do the Little Picture questions first. They can help you fill in the Big Picture.

## Little Picture Questions

More than two-thirds of Critical Reading questions ask about the Little Picture. Little Picture questions usually give you a line reference—a clue to where in the passage you'll find your answer.

Little Picture questions often:

- Test whether you understand significant information that's stated in the passage
- Ask you to make inferences or draw conclusions based on a part of the passage
- Ask you to relate parts of the passage to one another

Question three is a Little Picture question. Here's how you could solve it with the attack strategy.

> The "increased air space under the fur" mentioned in lines 5–6 serves primarily to
>
> (A) combat cold
>
> (B) intimidate other animals
>
> (C) render such measures obsolete
>
> (D) cool over-heated predators
>
> (E) make mammals more powerful

### 1. Read the Question Stem

Since the question is asking about a particular detail (it's just about the increased air space, not the passage as a whole), you know that this is a Little Picture question.

### 2. Locate the Material You Need

When you go back to the referenced line, you find that the increased air space "provides more effective insulation … allowing it to retain more heat."

### 3. Predict the Answer

It looks like the increased air space helps keep the animal warm.

## 4. Scan the Answer Choices

Beware of answer choices that provide a reasonable answer to the stem, but don't make sense in the context of the passage

(A) looks perfect.

(B) is tempting, since the raised fur also serves to make the animals look bigger and more intimidating.

(C) doesn't make too much sense in this context, and seems to be a distortion of the idea that goosebumps are obsolete.

(D) is actually the opposite of what you're looking for. This kind of wrong answer choice appears fairly often on the test.

(E) is also a distortion. Raised fur makes animals *appear* more powerful, but they are not actually more powerful.

## 5. Select Your Answer

You're left with (A) and (B). Be careful, though—the question is specifically asking about the increased air space, not raised fur in general. (A) refers to the air space, while (B) is more general. So, (A) is correct. Challenging Reading Comprehension questions force you to make *very* subtle distinctions.

## Vocabulary-in-Context Questions

Vocabulary-in-Context questions ask about the usage of a single word. These questions do not test your ability to define hard words like *archipelago* and *garrulous*. Instead, they test your ability to infer the meaning of a word from context. Words tested in SAT questions will probably be familiar to you—they are usually fairly common words with more than one definition. But that's the trick! Many of the answer choices will be definitions of the tested word, but only one will work in context. Vocabulary-in-Context questions always have a line reference, and you should always use it.

Sometimes one of the answer choices will jump out at you. It'll be the most common meaning of the word in question—but it's *rarely* right. You can think of this as the "obvious" choice. For example, say *curious* is the word being tested. The obvious choice is *inquisitive*. But curious also means *odd*, and that's more likely to be the answer.

Using context to find the answer will help prevent you from falling for this trap. You can use these choices to your advantage, though. If you get stuck on a Vocabulary-in-Context question, you can eliminate the "obvious" choice and guess.

Once you find the tested word in the passage, you should treat a Vocabulary-in-Context question like a Sentence Completion question. Pretend the word is a blank in the sentence. Read a line or two around the "blank," if you need to. Then predict a word for the "blank." Check the answer choices for a word that comes close to your prediction.

## EXTRA STRATEGIES FOR LONG PASSAGES

You use the same skills and strategies to tackle long passages as short passages—specifically Serious Skimming and the Five-Step Method. The subject matter and questions are also about the same for both passage types. The difference? With longer passages, you need to work harder to stay focused and organized. Here's how.

### Know the Question Order

Reading Comprehension questions have a specific order on longer passages: the first few questions ask about the beginning of the passage, the last few ask about the end.

### Read the Introduction

Each passage begins with a brief introduction. *Don't skip this part.* The introduction helps you focus your reading.

### Map It

Longer passages cover many different aspects of a topic. The first paragraph might introduce the subject, the second paragraph might present one viewpoint, and the third paragraph might argue for a different viewpoint. Within each of these paragraphs, there are several details that help the author convey a message.

Because there is a lot to keep track of, you need to mark up the passage as follows:

- Write simple notes in the margin as you read.
- Write down the purpose of each paragraph.
- Underline key points.
- Concentrate especially on places where the author expresses an opinion. Most Reading Comprehension questions hinge on opinions and viewpoints, not facts.

These notes are your Passage Map. The Passage Map helps you find the part of the passage that contains the information you need. The process of creating your Passage Map also forces you to read actively. This is especially helpful in the SAT's second and third hour, when you energy is flagging. Because you are constantly trying to identify the author's viewpoint and the purpose of each sentence and paragraph, you will be working hard to understand what's happening in the passage. This translates into points on the test.

### PASSAGE MAP

A good Passage Map should:

- Contain short words or phrases, not whole sentences
- Include markings in the passage like underlined and circled words
- Concentrate on viewpoints and opinions
- Note places where opinions other than the author's are expressed
- Avoid specific details

## Passage Map Practice

Write a Passage Map on this sample SAT passage, using the guidelines we just provided.

What a <u>marvelous and celestial</u> creature was    OP– L is <u>great</u>
Leonardo da Vinci. As a scientist and engineer,
his gifts were unparalleled. But his accomplish-
ment in these capacities was hindered by the fact
that he was, before all else, an artist. As one con-
versant with the (perfection of art) and knowing

the futility of trying to bring such perfection to the realm of practical application, Leonardo tended toward variability and inconstancy in his endeavors. His practice of moving compulsively from one project to the next, never bringing any of them to completion, stood in the way of his making any truly useful technical advances.

*MainPoint—L is genius, but never stuck w/1 thing long enuf 2B a "scientist"*

*OP – L underachieved*

When Leonardo was asked to create a memorial for one of his patrons, he designed a bronze horse of such vast proportions that it proved utterly impractical—even impossible—to produce. Some historians maintain that Leonardo never had any intention of finishing this work in the firstplace. But it is more likely that he simply became so intoxicated by his grand artistic conception that he lost sight of the fact that the monument actually had to be cast. Similarly, when Leonardo was commissioned to paint the *Last Supper*, he left the head of Christ unfinished, feeling incapable of investing it with a sufficiently divine demeanor. Yet, as a work of art rather than science or engineering, it is still worthy of our greatest veneration, for Leonardo succeeded brilliantly in capturing the acute anxiety of the Apostles at the most dramatic moment of the Passion narrative.

*Ex #1 – horse*

*alt. opinion*

*OP – L is a genius but impractical*

*Ex #2 – last Sup*

*MainPoint— L gets caught up in idea, forgets actual work*

Such mental restlessness, however, proved more problematic when applied to scientific matters. When he turned his mind to the natural world, Leonardo would begin by inquiring into the properties of herbs and end up observing the motions of the heavens. In his technical studies and scientific experiments, he would generate an endless stream of models and drawings, designing complex and unbuildable machines to raise great weights, bore through mountains, or even empty harbors.

*OP – switching from art to science here*

*Ex #1 – Natural*

*Ex #2 – technical*

*MainPoint L's short attention span bad for science*

It is this enormous intellectual fertility that has suggested to many that Leonardo can and should be regarded as one of the originators of modern science. But Leonardo was not himself a true scientist. "Science" is not the hundred-odd principles or *pensieri** that have been pulled out of his Codici. Science is comprehensive and methodical thought. Granted, Leonardo always became fascinated by the intricacies of specific technical challenges. He possessed the artist's interest in detail, which explains his compulsion with observation and problem solving. But such things alone do not constitute science, which requires the working out of a systematic body of knowledge—something Leonardo displayed little interest in doing.

*alt. opinion*

*OP*

*back?*

*MainPoint—L is genius and a compulsive problem-solver, but no scientist*

*L not good at*

* *thoughts*

Now take a look at our Passage Map notes. Did you highlight similar parts of the passage? Did you concentrate on the author's views?

## Paired Passages

Most SATs have at least one paired passage. A paired passage is two separate, shorter passages that each relate to the same topic. Questions following "paired passages" are generally ordered in this way: The first few questions relate to the first passage, the next few to the second passage, and the final questions ask about the passages as a pair.

Don't let the paired passages intimidate you—they're not twice as hard as the single reading selections. In fact, students often find the paired passages the most interesting selections on the test. Interesting, of course, relative to the rest of the SAT, not relative to, say, Beyoncé.

To tackle paired passages:

1. Skim Passage 1, looking for the drift (as you would with a single passage).

2. Do the question or questions that relate to the first passage.

3. Skim the second passage, looking for the drift and thinking about how the second passage relates to the first.

4. Do the question or questions that relate to the second passage.

5. Now you're ready to do the questions that ask about the relationship between the two passages.

Since you have to keep track of two different viewpoints with paired passages, it's especially important to read actively. Remember to ask yourself, "What are these passages about? What is each author's point? What is similar about the two passages? What is different?"

## When Time Is Running Out

We told you to save long passages for last, so you may often find yourself up against the clock. It's always best to skim the passage before you hit the questions. But if you only have a few minutes left, here's how to score points even while time is running out.

You can answer Vocabulary-in-Context questions and many Little Picture questions without reading the passage. If the question has a line reference, locate the material you need to find your answer and follow the Kaplan's Reading Comprehension Attack Strategy as usual. You won't have the overall picture to guide you, but you might be able to reach the correct answer just by understanding the "little picture."

Also, remember to skip around within the section if you need to. You can tackle the passages in any order you like within the same section. (But once you've read through the passage, try all the questions that go with it.)

## LONG PASSAGE PRACTICE

Test your reading skills on the following sample passages, keeping our tips and tactics in mind. Remember to read actively, and construct a Passage Map if that helps you. Then, use Kaplan's Attack Strategy to answer the questions that follow. Answers are on page 216.

**Questions 1–10 refer to the following passage.**

*In this essay, the author writes about her childhood on a Caribbean island that was an English colony for many years.*

When I saw England for the first time, I was a
child in school sitting at a desk. The England I
was looking at was laid out on a map gently,
beautifully, delicately, a very special jewel; it lay
5 on a bed of sky blue, its yellow form mysterious,
because though it looked like a leg of mutton*, it
could not really look like anything so familiar as
a leg of mutton because it was England. England
was a special jewel all right, and only special peo-
10 ple got to wear it. The people who got to wear
England were English people. They wore it well
and they wore it everywhere: in jungles, in
deserts, on plains, in places where they were not
welcome, in places they should not have been.
15 When my teacher had pinned this map up on the
blackboard, she said, "This is England"—and she
said it with authority, seriousness, and adoration,
and we all sat up. We understood then—we were
meant to understand then—that England was to
20 be our source of myth and the source from
which we got our sense of reality, our sense of
what was meaningful, our sense of what was
meaningless—and much about our own lives
and much about the very idea of us headed that
25 last list.

At the time I was a child sitting at my desk
seeing England for the first time, I was already
very familiar with the greatness of it. Each morning before I left for school, I ate a breakfast of
30 half a grapefruit, a bowl of oat porridge, bread
and butter and a slice of cheese, and a cup of
cocoa. The can of cocoa was often left on the

table in front of me. It had written on it the
name of the company, the year the company was
35 established, and the words "Made in England."
Those words, "Made in England," were written
on the box the oats came in too. The shoes I
wore were made in England; so were my socks
and cotton undergarments and the satin ribbons
40 I wore tied at the end of two plaits of my hair.
My father, who might have sat next to me at
breakfast, was a carpenter and cabinet maker.
The shoes he wore to work would have been
made in England, as were his khaki shirt and
45 trousers, his underpants and undershirt, his
socks and brown felt hat. Felt was not the proper
material from which a hat that was expected to
provide shade from the hot sun should be made,
but my father must have seen and admired a pic-
50 ture of an Englishman wearing such a hat in
England. As we sat at breakfast a car might go by.
The car, a Hillman or a Zephyr, was made in
England. The very conception of the meal itself,
breakfast, and its substantial quality and quantity
55 was an idea from England; we somehow knew
that in England they began the day with this
meal called breakfast and a proper breakfast was
a big breakfast.

At the time I saw this map—seeing England
60 for the first time—I did not say to myself, "Ah, so
that's what it looks like," because there was no
longing in me to put a shape to those three
words that ran through every part of my life, no
matter how small; for me to have had such a
65 longing would have meant that I lived in a certain atmosphere, an atmosphere in which those
three words were felt as a burden. But I did not
live in such an atmosphere. My father's brown

felt hat would develop a hole in its crown, the
70 lining would separate from the hat itself, and six
weeks before he thought that he could not be
seen wearing it—he was a very vain man—he
would order another hat from England. And my
mother taught me to eat my food in the English
75 way: the knife in the right hand, the fork in the
left, my elbows held still close to my side. When I
had finally mastered it, I overheard her saying to
a friend, "Did you see how nicely she can eat?"
But I knew then that I enjoyed my food more
80 when I ate it with my bare hands, and I contin-
ued to do so when she wasn't looking. And when
my teacher showed us the map, she asked us to
study it carefully, because no test we would ever
take would be complete without this statement:
85 "Draw a map of England."

I did not know then that the statement "Draw
a map of England" was something far worse than
a declaration of war. I did not know then that
this statement was part of a process that would
90 result in my erasure, not my physical erasure, but
my erasure all the same. I did not know then that
this statement was meant to make me feel in awe
and small whenever I heard the word "England":
awe at its existence, small because I was not from
95 it. I did not know very much of anything then—
certainly not what a blessing it was that I was
unable to draw a map of England correctly.

*the flesh of a sheep

1. According to the author, England could not really look like a leg of mutton (line 6) because

   (A) maps generally don't give an accurate impression of what a place looks like

   (B) England was too grand and exotic a place for such a mundane image

   (C) England was an island not very different in appearance from her own island

   (D) the usual metaphor used to describe England was a precious jewel

   (E) mutton was one of the few foods familiar to her that did not come from England

2. The author's reference to felt as "not the proper material" (lines 46–47) for her father's hat chiefly serves to emphasize her point about the

   (A) extremity of the local weather

   (B) arrogance of island laborers

   (C) informality of dress on the island

   (D) weakness of local industries

   (E) predominance of English culture

3. The word "conception" as used in line 53 most nearly means

   (A) beginning

   (B) image

   (C) origination

   (D) notion

   (E) plan

4. The word "substantial" in line 54 most nearly means
   (A) important
   (B) abundant
   (C) firm
   (D) down-to-earth
   (E) materialistic

5. In the third paragraph, the author implies that any longing to put a shape to the words "Made in England" would have indicated
   (A) a resentment of England's predominance
   (B) an unhealthy desire to become English
   (C) an inability to understand England's authority
   (D) an excessive curiosity about England
   (E) an unfamiliarity with English customs

6. The author cites the anecdotes about her father and mother in lines 68–78 primarily to convey their
   (A) love for their children
   (B) belief in strict discipline
   (C) distaste for anything foreign
   (D) reverence for England
   (E) overemphasis on formal manners

7. The word "erasure" (lines 90–91) as used by the author most nearly means

   (A) total annihilation

   (B) physical disappearance

   (C) sense of insignificance

   (D) enforced censorship

   (E) loss of freedom

8. The main purpose of the passage is to

   (A) advocate a change in the way a subject is taught in school

   (B) convey the personality of certain figures from the author's childhood

   (C) describe an overwhelming influence on the author's early life

   (D) analyze the importance of a sense of place to early education

   (E) relate a single formative episode in the author's life

9. For the author, the requirement to "draw a map of England" (line 46) represented an attempt to
   (A) force students to put their studies to practical use
   (B) glorify one culture at the expense of another
   (C) promote an understanding of world affairs
   (D) encourage students to value their own heritage
   (E) impart outmoded and inappropriate knowledge

10. At the end of the passage, the author suggests that her inability "to draw a map of England correctly" indicated a
   (A) heartfelt desire to see the country in person rather than through maps
   (B) serious failure of the education she received
   (C) conscious rejection of the prestige of a foreign power
   (D) harmful preoccupation with local affairs and customs
   (E) beneficial ignorance of her own supposed inferiority

**Questions 11–15 refer to the following passage.**

*In this essay, the author writes about the role of television and the question of audience in the contemporary courtroom. The following are excerpts from a speech about this issue given by a retired Chief Judge of New York State at a Pre-law Association meeting.*

Justice is the most profound aspiration of men and women on earth; it is the allotment to each person of that to which he or she is entitled; it exists only when there has been adherence to
5 principles of honesty and fairness and disregard of other considerations.

Down through the centuries, the character of a particular government or civilization could be measured best by the sort of justice meted out to
10 its citizens. In the more advanced and more humane governances, trials have taken place in courtrooms to which the public has been admitted. On the other hand, secret trials have almost invariably been the telltale sign of oppressive and
15 autocratic regimes. Indeed, the grant of a fair trial is the greatest contribution of any jurisprudence.

The difference in openness is not without significance. It is not a matter of mere entertainment. It is far more serious than that. First, and
20 foremost, unobstructed courtrooms are a guarantee of fairness and justice. Furthermore, the public officials functioning therein can be observed so that those performing well may be retained and those not may be replaced.

25 Courtrooms with "open doors" have always been a fetish for me. I stood here in this city sixteen years ago and in an interview announced that I favored cameras in the courts. Broadcasting from courtrooms was unpopular
30 then and there were only four states in the Union permitting television of judicial proceedings. My

response shocked many in this state. When the
Chief Judgeship came my way, a rule was adopt-
ed permitting television and still cameras in the
35 appellate courts of our jurisdiction and it was a
success. I worked long and hard in favor of an
amendment of the Civil Rights Law to allow
photography in the trial courts. I am pleased that
that is now reality.
40 However, I am worried. I am worried about
what seems to be an increasing antipathy toward
the media and concurrent attempts to narrow
the doors leading into courtrooms by distin-
guishing ancillary or supplemental proceedings
45 from trials themselves. Freedom of the press and
open courtrooms go together.
I believe in the First Amendment. I believe
with might and main in the constitutional guarantee of freedom of the press, not merely to curry
50 favor with those of the "Fourth Estate," not merely as an aid to the media in its varied shapes and
forms, but more as a benefit for all the people. A
broadly defined freedom of the press assures the
maintenance of our political system of democra-
55 cy, social equality, and public exposure. Indeed,
the strength of America, different from any
nation in the world, lies in its openness.

11. In line 17, the word "openness" most nearly
means

(A) candor
(B) tolerance
(C) receptivity
(D) friendliness
(E) accessibility

12. The information in lines 40–46 suggests that the judge is very concerned about

   (A) restrictions being placed upon people opposed to media participation in the judicial process

   (B) undermining the rights of the accused by giving the media too much access to the judicial process

   (C) media abuse of the First Amendment to distort the judicial process

   (D) harm being caused to the judicial process by a distaste for the media

   (E) encouraging those who favor a narrow definition of civil rights by allowing the media to participate in the judicial process

13. The judge's point about the role of the media in the judicial process is made mainly through

   (A) general statements

   (B) specific examples

   (C) statistical data

   (D) long citations

   (E) scientific evidence

14. In lines 47–57, the judge reflects on the
    (A) strengths and weaknesses of the judicial
        system
    (B) attitude of the judicial system toward the
        media
    (C) role of a free press in maintaining a demo-
        cratic society
    (D) ability of the media to function effectively
        in the courtroom
    (E) connection between the First Amendment
        and the Civil Rights Law

15. Which best describes the judge's view of
    cameras in the courtroom?
    (A) Cameras do not play a useful part in
        determining which members of the
        judicial system are competent and
        which members are incompetent.
    (B) While the First Amendment gives the
        media the right to bring cameras into
        the courtroom, their use has impaired
        the proper functioning of the judicial
        system.
    (C) Judicial systems that allow cameras into
        the courtroom are no more likely to be
        fair than judicial systems which do not
        admit them.
    (D) Regardless of the fact that many members
        of the judicial system do not approve of
        their presence, cameras should be per-
        mitted in every courtroom.
    (E) Oppressive and autocratic regimes are
        likely to place cameras in the court-
        room to deter their subjects from com-
        mitting criminal acts.

## REMEMBER...

The two most important skills in the Reading Comprehension section are (1) to read with a purpose and (2) to figure out the meaning of unfamiliar words from context.

Reading Comprehension questions are based on two types of passages—short passages (100–150 words) and long passages (400–850 words).

Reading Comprehension questions are NOT ordered by difficulty.

You should *seriously skim* reading passages, instead of reading them word-for-word.

Once you have seriously skimmed the passage, use Kaplan's Reading Comprehension Attack Strategy to:

1. Read the question stem.
2. Locate the material you need.
3. Predict the answer.
4. Scan the answer choices.
5. Select your answer.

Most Reading Comprehension questions fall into three basic types.

- "Big Picture" questions test your overall understanding of the passage's biggest points.
- "Little Picture" questions ask about localized bits of information.
- Vocabulary-in-Context questions ask for the meaning of a single word.

It's important to stay focused when reading long passages.

Create a Passage Map that includes:

- Notes in the margin
- Purpose of each paragraph
- Key points underlined
- Emphasis on author opinions

Approach paired passages the same way you approach single passages.

If your time is running out, answer Vocabulary-in-Context and Little Picture questions first.

# ANSWERS AND EXPLANATIONS

## Short Passages

**1. C**

Choose which answer best describes what the author thinks about the little boy. A specific line reference is given, so refer back to the passage. You will see that the author does not recognize a scared little boy in himself, therefore the correct answer choice is (C) as he has changed considerably since childhood.

**2. B**

Context clues from lines 12–14 include the word "shrewd" and the inference that selling heat would "surely bring fortune." Although choice (A) is certainly true of the passage, it is not specifically referred to in the lines mentioned in the question. There was no mention of the cold being an obstacle or of it being unimportant.

**3. A**

This is a Little Picture question. Refer to the lines mentioned in the question. If you keep reading the following sentence, it clearly states that "the air space provides more effective insulation for the mammal's body, thus allowing it to retain more heat for longer periods of time."

**4. D**

Although the answer is not stated explicitly in the passage, there are some clues to the answer. Choice (A) is incorrect because the passage mentions the need for goosebumps (insulation) and how they occur. Although goosebumps may occur during frightening experiences, there in nothing in the passage that implies that they are harmful—choice (B). Goosebumps may be a funny name for something that may occur as a reaction to danger, but there is nothing in the passage to imply that goosebumps are dangerous—choice (C). Nothing in the passage mentions the power or the frequency of goosebumps, therefore choice (E) is incorrect.

**5. D**

The answer to this question can be found in lines 7–9. The author writes, "Aurora Leigh is not a traditional Victorian woman—she is well-educated and self-sufficient." This statement sets up the contrast between Aurora, who is well-educated, and the traditional Victorian woman, who is not well-educated.

**6. C**

The word "effect" is both a noun and a verb, so you must look at its use in the sentence to determine its part of speech and meaning. The word is used in the phrase "to rise up and effect a change." If you are unclear of the meaning, try inserting the answer choices in the sentence to see if it makes sense: to *imitate* a change, to *result* a change, to *cause* a change, to *disturb* a change, to *prevent* a change. Although you may have been tempted to choose (B), result, thinking that effect is a noun, the only answer choice that makes sense in the context of the sentence is choice (C), cause.

## Long Passages

**1. B**

By scanning the answer choices and by reading the material surrounding the reference in the question (line 6), you can find the answer. In lines 7–10, the author states, "it could not really look like anything so familiar as a leg of mutton…England was a special jewel…and only special people got to wear it." Only answer choice (B) is supported by the text.

**2. E**

To find the correct answer, you must read the context of the statement referenced in the question. When the author states that felt is "not the proper material," you may be tempted to choose answer (B) which mentions arrogance, or (C), informality. Refer back to the passage. Lines 47–51 mention that felt was not proper because it could not provide protection from the sun. This may cause you to think that choice (A) is correct because of the comment about the weather. However, if you keep reading, the author mentions that her "father must have seen and admired…an Englishman wearing such a hat in England." This supports choice (E) as the correct answer.

**3. D**

Use context clues to determine the answer. Refer back to the passage and if necessary, replace "conception" with the answer choices to find the best meaning of the word. "The very conception of the meal itself, breakfast, […] was an idea from England." Although "beginning" and "origination" seem to fit in the context of the sentence, only "notion," or idea, most nearly means "conception."

**4. B**

For this question, try replacing "substantial" as it is used in the sentence, with each of the answer choices. For example, "[…] its substantial quality and quantity was an idea from England": its *important* quality, its *abundant* quality, its *firm* quality, its *down-to-earth* quality, its *materialistic* quality. Even if you don't know the meaning of the word abundant, answer choice (B) makes the most sense in the context of the sentence.

**5. B**

You should reread the third paragraph to get a sense of the tone of the question. If you scan the answer choices, most of them imply something negative: resentment, unhealthy, inability, excessive, unfamiliarity. In lines 66–67, the author states, "those three words were felt as a burden." Lines 79–80 also mention that she "enjoyed [her] food more when I ate it with my bare hands." These things imply that the author did *not* have a desire to become English.

**6. D**

Throughout the passage, the author is commenting on her parents' love for England and its traditions. The anecdotes refer to their behavior relating to English custom, so the author is conveying her parents' reverence for England.

**7. C**

Read the lines referenced in the question. The author talks about a "process that would result in my erasure, not my physical erasure, but my erasure all the same." The context eliminates choices (A) and (B) since she is not physically disappearing or being destroyed. The context mentions nothing of censorship nor of freedom. Therefore, the best choice is (C), her sense of insignificance.

**8. C**

Read through the answer choices. The passage does not mention how subjects are taught in school—choice (A), nor does it specifically mention the personalities of certain figures in her childhood—choice (B). Although the passage does mention the importance of a sense of place, it is not related to early education. This passage does mention several episodes from her life, which rules out choice (E). The main purpose of the passage is to describe an influence in the author's early life.

**9. B**

Drawing a map of England did not encourage students to value their own heritage, promote an understanding of world affairs, nor to learn inappropriate knowledge. Although you might be tempted by choice (A), within the context of the passage, drawing a map of England was a way of glorifying one culture at the expense of another.

**10. E**

There is nothing in the passage to indicate that choices (A) or (D) is correct. Although she did not know how to draw a map of England, she does not indicate that it was a conscious rejection—choice (C)—or a failure of her education—choice (B). The best answer is choice (E).

**11. E**

As used in paragraph 5, *openness* refers to the discussion in paragraph 2 about whether the public can be admitted to the courtroom. (E) *accessibility* best defines this sense of openness.

The other choices are all possible meanings of openness, but none fits the context. (A) candor, or frankness, refers to openness of one's own opinions; (B) tolerance is openness to other people or their views; (C) receptivity implies a willingness to be convinced. (D) friendliness suggests an outgoing nature, which doesn't match what the author is saying here.

**12. D**

In paragraph 7, the author worries over "antipathy," or dislike, toward the media. This is paraphrased as distaste in (D). The harm . . . to the judicial process in this answer choice arises from the author's strong belief that media access is good for the judicial process.

If you know the author favors cameras, or media participation, you're likely to pick the right answer. The other four choices, in different ways, say the author worries about too much media participation; they contradict the author's point of view.

**13. A**

Paragraphs 1–3 and paragraph 6 all contain broad arguments about the nature of justice, the need for public trials, and the importance of freedom of the press—(A) *general statements*. The author gives no (B) *specific examples* of how courtroom openness works, though there is one example of the author's own activity (paragraph 4). The passage never uses (C) *statistics* or (E) *scientific findings*, and never refers to *judicial decisions or other writings or speeches* (D).

**14. C**

This question asks about paragraph 6, which discusses *freedom of the press* and its importance in upholding democracy, equality, and other American values (C).

The passage discusses the attitude of the judicial system to the media, so you might be tempted by (B). But this isn't a Big Picture question; you're asked to focus only on certain lines. Similarly, (A) is discussed only in paragraph 2. And while paragraph 6 mentions (E) the *First Amendment*, it never mentions the *Civil Rights Law*. Finally, (D) how the *media function* in the courtroom is never discussed.

**15. D**

You need to describe the overall point of view here. Since the author strongly supports cameras in the courts, and the whole passage defends this view, your answer must be (D), the only pro-camera choice. (D) acknowledges the opposition to cameras noted in paragraph 5, but says this opposition should be disregarded—as the author implies, too (paragraph 6).

Choice (A) contradicts a minor point the author raises in the last part of paragraph 3. (B) distorts what paragraph 6 says about the First Amendment, as well as the author's pro-media position. (C) contradicts the general sense of paragraph 2, though cameras are not specifically discussed there. (E) refers to the discussion of oppressive regimes in this same paragraph, but the author never raises this point.

# Chapter Nine: **Strategies for SAT Sentence Completion Questions**

- **Using Context Clues**
- **Avoiding Tricky Wrong Answers**
- **Working Around Tough Vocabulary**

Sentence Completion questions are probably the Critical Reading section's most student-friendly question type. Unlike the Reading Comprehension questions that make up the bulk of this section, Sentence Completion questions require you to pay attention to just one sentence at a time.

## KNOW THE DIRECTIONS

The instructions for Sentence Completion questions are as follows.

**Directions:** Select the lettered word or set of words that best completes the sentence.

The questions look like this:

Today's small, portable computers contrast markedly with the earliest electronic computers, which were - - - - .

(A) effective

(B) invented

(C) useful

(D) destructive

(E) enormous

In this example, the new, small, portable computers are contrasted with old computers. You can infer that old computers must be the opposite of small and portable, so (E), *enormous*, is the right answer.

As you can see, to answer Sentence Completion questions, you need to determine the relationship between the parts of the sentence to figure out which word gives the sentence its intended meaning. We'll show you how to do this.

### ORDER OF DIFFICULTY

Sentence Completion questions will likely be arranged in order of difficulty. We say "likely," because as of this printing, that information has not been released by the College Board. Based on the format of the old SAT, however, we expect that the easier questions will appear first in the section, the medium questions in the middle, and the hardest questions at the end.

## KAPLAN'S SENTENCE COMPLETION ATTACK STRATEGY

This is Kaplan's attack strategy for tackling Sentence Completion questions. If you can master these, you will be on your way to a higher score.

1. Read the sentence for clue words.
2. Predict the answer.
3. Select the best match.
4. Plug your answer choice into the sentence.

### 1. Read the Sentence for Clue Words

Read the sentence. Now think about the sentence for five seconds. Take special note of the clue words. A word like *but* tells you to expect a CONTRAST in the next part of the sentence; a word like *moreover* tells you that what follows is a CONTINUATION of the same idea. Clue words such as *and, but, such as, however,* and *although* tell you how the parts of the sentence will relate to each other.

## 2. Predict the Answer

Decide what sort of word should fill the blank or blanks. Do this BEFORE looking at the answer choices. You don't have to guess the *exact* word; a rough idea of the *kind* of word you need will do. It's often enough to simply predict whether the missing word is positive or negative. But often you will be able to go farther. For example, you may be able to predict whether you need a pair of synonyms to fill in the blanks or two words that contrast.

## 3. Select the Best Match

Compare your prediction to each answer choice. Read EVERY answer choice before deciding which answer best completes the sentence.

## 4. Plug Your Answer Choice into the Sentence

Put your answer choice in the blank (or blanks). Only one choice should really make sense. If you've gone through the four steps and more than one choice still looks good, eliminate the choice(s) that you can, guess from the remaining choices, and move on. If all of the choices look great or all of the choices look terrible, circle the question and come back to it when you've finished the section.

Let's unleash the powers of Kaplan's Sentence Completion Attack Strategy on a sample question.

> The king's - - - - decisions as a diplomat and administrator led to his legendary reputation as a just and - - - - ruler.
>
> (A) quick . . capricious
>
> (B) equitable . . wise
>
> (C) immoral . . perceptive
>
> (D) generous . . witty
>
> (E) clever . . uneducated

## 1. Read the Sentence for Clue Words

The clues here are the phrase *led to* and the word *just*. You know that the kind of decisions the king made *led to* him having a reputation as a just and - - - - ruler. So whatever goes in both blanks must be consistent with *just*.

## 2. Predict the Answer

Both blanks must contain words that are similar in meaning. Because of his - - - - decisions, the king is viewed as a just and - - - - ruler. So if the king's decisions were good, he'd be remembered as a good ruler, and if his decisions were bad, he'd be remembered as a bad ruler.

*Just*, which means "fair," is a positive-sounding word; therefore, you can predict that both blanks will be similar in meaning and that both will be positive words. You can write a plus sign in the blanks or over the columns of answer choices to remind you.

## 3. Select the Best Match

One effective way to choose the best answer is to determine which answers have the kinds of words you predicted—in this case, words that are both positive and synonymous. In (A), *quick* and *capricious* are not necessarily positive, and they are not similar in meaning. (*Capricious* means erratic or fickle.) In (B), *equitable* means fair. *Equitable* and *wise* are similar, and they're both positive. When you plug them in, they make sense, so (B) looks right. But check out the others to be sure. In (C), *immoral* and *perceptive* are not similar at all; moreover, *perceptive* is positive, but *immoral* is not. In (D), *generous* and *witty* are both positive adjectives, but they are not very similar, and they don't make sense in the sentence; *generous* decisions would not give one a reputation as a *witty* ruler. In (E), *clever* and *uneducated* aren't similar, and *clever* is positive, but *uneducated* isn't. Thus, (B) is the best match.

## 4. Plug your Answer Choice into the Sentence

*The king's equitable decisions as a diplomat and administrator led to his legendary reputation as a just and wise ruler.* Choice (B) makes sense in the sentence and is the correct answer.

## CLUE WORDS IN DEPTH

To do well on Sentence Completion questions, you need to understand how the parts of a sentence fit together to create meaning. Clue words help you do this. The more clues you uncover, the clearer the sentence becomes, and the better you can predict what goes in the blanks. So let's delve further into the fascinating subject of clue words. Take a look at this example.

Though some have derided it as - - - - , the
search for extraterrestrial intelligence has actually
become a respectable scientific endeavor.

Here, the word *though* is an important clue. *Though sets up a* contrast between the way some have derided (belittled or ridiculed) the
search for extraterrestrial intelligence and the fact that the scientific
endeavor has become respectable. Another important clue is *actually*.
*Actually* completes the contrast: Though some think the endeavor
ridiculous, the reality is that it has become respectable.

These clues tell you that whatever goes in the blank must complete
the contrast implied by the word *though*. Therefore, to fill in the
blank, you need a word that would be used to describe the opposite
of "a respectable scientific endeavor." *Foolish* or *trivial* would be good
predictions for the blank.

Let's put your deeper understanding of clue words to the test. Use
clue words to predict the answers to the two questions below. First,
look at the sentences without the answer choices and:

- Circle clue words.
- Think of a word or phrase that might go in each blank.
- Write your prediction below each sentence.

1. One striking aspect of Caribbean music is its
   - - - - of many African musical - - - - , such as
   call-and-response singing and polyrhythms.

Predictions: _____ _____

2. Although Cézanne was inspired by the
   Impressionists, he - - - - their emphasis on the
   effects of light and - - - - an independent
   approach to painting that emphasized form.

Predictions: _____ _____

Here are the questions with their answer choices (and with their clue words italicized). Find the right answer to each question, referring to the predictions you just made.

1. One striking aspect of Caribbean music is its
   - - - - of many African musical - - - - , *such as*
   call-and-response singing and polyrhythms.

   (A) recruitment .. groups

   (B) proficiency .. events

   (C) expectation .. ideas

   (D) absorption .. forms

   (E) condescension .. priorities

2. *Although* Cézanne was inspired by the
   Impressionists, he - - - - their emphasis on the
   effects of light and - - - - an independent
   approach to painting that emphasized form.

   (A) accepted .. developed

   (B) rejected .. evolved

   (C) encouraged .. submerged

   (D  dismissed .. aborted

   (E) nurtured .. founded

The answers to the questions are (D) and (B), respectively. In question 1, *such as* tells you that the second blank must be something (genres, practices, or forms) of which call-and-response singing and polyrhythms are examples. *Although* in question 2 tells you that the first blank must contrast with Cézanne's being *inspired* by the Impressionists.

## GETTING THE HARD QUESTIONS RIGHT

It is likely that Sentence Completion questions will go from easiest to hardest—the higher the question number, the harder the question, so the last few Sentence Completion questions in a set are usually pretty difficult.

If you find yourself getting stuck, we have a few special techniques to pull you through:

- Avoid tricky wrong answers.
- Take apart tough sentences.
- Work around tough vocabulary.

## Avoid Tricky Wrong Answers

Toward the end of a set, watch out for tricky answer choices. Avoid:

- Opposites of the correct answer
- Words that sound right because they're hard
- Two-blankers in which one word fits but the other doesn't

Take a look at the following example.

> Granted that Janyce is extremely - - - -; still, it is difficult to imagine her as a professional comedian.
>
> (A) dull
>
> (B) garrulous
>
> (C) effusive
>
> (D) conservative
>
> (E) witty

Read this sentence carefully or you may get tricked. If you read too quickly, you might think, "If Janyce is hard to imagine as a comedian, she's probably extremely dull or conservative. So I'll pick either (A) or (D)." But the sentence is saying something else.

Remember to pick up the clues. The key here is the clue word *granted*, which is another way of saying *although*. So the sentence means, "Sure Janyce is funny, but she's no professional comedian." Therefore, the word in the blank must resemble "funny." That means (E), *witty*, is correct. *Still* is another important clue word that emphasizes the contrast between how Janyce is (witty) and imagining her as a comedian.

Now don't pick an answer just because it sounds hard. *Garrulous* means talkative and *effusive* means overly expressive. You might be tempted to pick one of these simply because they sound impressive.

But they're put on the test just to trick you. Don't choose them without good reason.

Now let's look at a two-blank sentence.

> When the state government discovered that thermal pollution was killing valuable fish, legislation was passed to - - - - the dumping of hot liquid wastes into rivers and to - - - - the fish population.
>
> (A) discourage . . decimate
>
> (B) regulate . . quantify
>
> (C) facilitate . . appease
>
> (D) discontinue . . devastate
>
> (E) prohibit . . protect

Look at all the choices. Check out the first blank first. Legislation was not passed to *facilitate* dumping, so that eliminates choice (C). The other four are all possible.

Now check the second blanks. The legislature wouldn't pass a law to *decimate*, *quantify*, or *devastate* the fish population, so (A), (B), and (D) are wrong. Only choice (E), *prohibit . . protect*, fits for both blanks. The legislature might well pass a law to *prohibit* dumping hot liquids and to *protect* fish.

## Take Apart Tough Sentences

Some sentences are difficult because they seem to lack the context you need to determine the correct answer. For example, look at the following sentence.

> Although this small and selective publishing
> house is famous for its - - - - standards, sever-
> al of its recent novels have appealed to the
> general public.
>
> (A) proletarian
> (B) naturalistic
> (C) discriminating
> (D) imitative
> (E) precarious

In this sentence, the parts of the sentence surrounding the blank
seem a little vague, and the word choices are slightly advanced adjectives. What sort of publishing house is it? The answer here is not clear
right off the bat. But what if you were stumped and had no idea
which word to pick or what the meaning of all of the words were?
Sometimes the only thing to do in this situation is to plug in the
answer choices and make the best guess based on which word you
think gives the most information. Here, we are looking for a word that
describes standards that would keep them from publishing books that
appeal to the general public.

(A) *Proletarian* standards? Hmmm . . . doesn't seem appropriate.
*Proletarian* means characteristic of the average citizen or working
class, so, in fact, it's the opposite of what we need.

(B) *Naturalistic* standards? Not great. It doesn't seem to contrast with
the idea of popular appeal.

(C) *Discriminating* standards? Seems to fit. If they are discriminating,
they are very selective and would probably not publish books that are
popular with the general public.

(D) *Imitative* standards? Sounds weird and doesn't really make sense.

(E) *Precarious* standards? Nope. Again, it doesn't make sense in the
context of the sentence, whatever kind of publisher it is.

Choice (C) sounds best and, as it turns out, is correct. Although the
small publishing house has *discriminating*, or picky, standards, several
of its recent novels appeal to a general audience.

Now try a complex sentence with two blanks. Use these two important guidelines:

- Try the easier blank first.
- Save time by eliminating all choices that won't work for one blank.

The following example is the fifth question out of a nine-problem set.

> These latest employment statistics from the present administration are so loosely documented, carelessly explained, and potentially misleading that even the most loyal senators will - - - - the - - - - of the presidential appointees who produced them.
>
> (A) perceive . . intelligence
>
> (B) understand . . tenacity
>
> (C) recognize . . incompetence
>
> (D) praise . . rigor
>
> (E) denounce . . loyalty

It's not so easy to see what goes in the first blank, so try the second blank. You need a word to describe presidential appointees who produced the *loosely documented, carelessly explained, and misleading* statistics. Based on these key words, we know that the second blank must be negative. The only second-word answer choice that's definitely negative is (C), *incompetence*, or inability to perform a task. Now try *recognize* in the first blank. It fits, too. (C) must be correct. See how much time you save? This step safely eliminates all choices except the correct answer.

## Work Around Tough Vocabulary

Fortunately, you can often figure out enough context to get the correct answer, even if you don't know all of the vocabulary words in the sentence. That's because test developers often provide other clues to help you figure out the intended meaning. Look at the following sentence as an example.

> Despite her - - - - of public speaking experi-
> ence, the student council member was sur-
> prisingly cogent, and expressed the concerns
> of her classmates persuasively.
>
> (A) hope
> (B) depth
> (C) method
> (D) lack
> (E) union

If you don't know what *cogent* means, work around it. From the sentence, especially the clue word *and*, you know that *cogent* goes with
"expressed the concerns of her classmates persuasively." So you don't
have to worry about what *cogent* means. All you need to know is that
the student council member was persuasive despite a - - - - of speaking experience. *Surprisingly* is another clue. It suggests that the student was not expected to express herself so effectively because she
did not have much public speaking experience. Further, two of the
answer choices don't really make sense if you insert them in the
blank—a *method* or *union* of speaking experience? It can't be.

Only (D), *lack*, fits the context. *Despite her lack of public speaking
experience, the student council member expressed the concerns of
her classmates persuasively.* (By the way, *cogent* means *convincing,
believable,* roughly the same as "expressing concern persuasively.")

Let's look at another Sentence Completion question. This time the
tough vocabulary is in the answer choices.

> Advances in technology occur at such a fast
> pace that dictionaries have difficulty incorpo-
> rating the - - - - that emerge for new inven-
> tions.
>
> (A) colloquialisms
> (B) euphemisms
> (C) compensations
> (D) neologisms
> (E) clichés

Whatever goes in the blank has to describe the "new inventions." If you don't know what all of these words mean, don't give up. Rule out as many choices as you can, and guess among the remaining ones.

You can eliminate (C) and (E)—words that you are probably familiar with—right off the bat. They don't describe new inventions and wouldn't be put in a dictionary. Now you can make an educated guess. Remember, educated guessing will help your score more than guessing blindly or skipping the question. So use your knowledge of prefixes, suffixes, word roots, and foreign languages to try to rule out one or more of the remaining choices.

For example, you might know that *neo* means "new," so the word *neologisms* might be the best choice for something that gets put in a dictionary and describes new inventions. In fact, it's the right answer (D). *Neologisms* are newly coined words. (Don't forget to check out Chapter 10: Building Your Vocabulary to review roots.)

## If All Else Fails—Guess!

If you're really stumped, don't be afraid to guess. Eliminate all answer choices that seem wrong and guess from the remaining choices. If you have eliminated at least one or two choices, the chance to gain points outweighs the possibility of losing points for incorrect answers.

Now take a deep breath, then practice the strategies you've learned on this Sentence Completion question set.

## SENTENCE COMPLETION PRACTICE

**Directions:** For each question in this section, select the best answer from among the choices given. Check your answers on page 240.

1. Soon after adopting a syllabic system of writing, the Greeks made the final step to a phonetic alphabet, dividing the consonants from the vowels and writing each - - - - .

   (A) formally
   (B) abstractly
   (C) separately
   (D) mysteriously
   (E) accurately

2. The stranger was actually smaller than I thought; his stature was - - - - by the alarm he caused as he loomed up suddenly in the dark alley.

   (A) worsened
   (B) magnified
   (C) disparaged
   (D) disfigured
   (E) admonished

3. Although the risk of a nuclear accident remained - - - - , the public's concern about such an accident gradually - - - - .

   (A) steady . . waned
   (B) acute . . persisted
   (C) unclear . . shifted
   (D) obvious . . endured
   (E) pressing . . remained

4. Prior to the American entrance into World War I, President Woodrow Wilson strove to maintain the - - - - of the United States, warning both sides against encroachments on American interests.

   (A) involvement
   (B) belligerence
   (C) versatility
   (D) magnanimity
   (E) neutrality

5. The graceful curves of the colonial-era buildings that dominated the old part of the city contrasted sharply with the modern, - - - - subway stations and made the latter appear glaringly out of place.

   (A) festive
   (B) grimy
   (C) angular
   (D) gigantic
   (E) efficient

6. Bird species - - - - to this island were exterminated by feral cats, - - - - of pets abandoned
here decades ago by sailors.

(A) provincial . . competitors

(B) harmless . . liberators

(C) indigenous . . descendants

(D) unusual . . signals

(E) benign . . ancestors

7. Unfortunately, the treasurer's plan to get the
company out of debt - - - - gaining access to
certain funds that may never become available.

(A) speaks to

(B) treats with

(C) delves into

(D) metes out

(E) hinges on

8. Based on factual - - - - rather than conjecture,
Dr. Singh's report will - - - - previously held
views about the nesting habits of the rare
species.

(A) conjecture . . ignore

(B) evidence . . refute

(C) theory . . negate

(D) projections . . corroborate

(E) documentation . . inspire

9. Gary was - - - - about the - - - - of his family
   heirlooms and personal mementos in the fire.

   (A) depressed . . meaning

   (B) noncommittal . . eradication

   (C) incensed . . recovery

   (D) mournful . . insurance

   (E) distraught . . destruction

10. Many novels by the Brontë sisters and other
    19th century female authors were initially pub-
    lished under masculine - - - - in the belief that
    works by - - - - authors would meet more
    favorable reception.

    (A) monikers . . patriarchal

    (B) aliases . . established

    (C) rubrics . . famous

    (D) pseudonyms . . male

    (E) criteria . . talented

11. In 1883, - - - - eruption of Mount Krakatoa
    killed many thousands of people and - - - -
    havoc on the coasts of Java and Sumatra.

    (A) a fateful . . diminished

    (B) an inoffensive . . spawned

    (C) an immoral . . reigned

    (D) a blistering . . authorized

    (E) a disastrous . . wreaked

12. The discovery of the Dead Sea Scrolls in the
    1940s quickly - - - - the popular imagination,
    but the precise significance of the scrolls is still
    - - - - by scholars.

    (A) impressed . . understood

    (B) alarmed . . obscured

    (C) troubled . . perceived

    (D) sparked . . disputed

    (E) eluded . . debated

13. In Kafka's characteristically surreal story "The
    Hunger Artist," the main character "entertains"
    the public by starving himself until he is too
    - - - - to survive.

    (A) glutted

    (B) lachrymose

    (C) emaciated

    (D) superfluous

    (E) satiated

14. Recent editions of the Chinese classic *Tao Te
    Ching*, based on manuscripts more authoritative
    than those hitherto available, have rendered
    previous editions - - - - .

    (A) incomprehensible

    (B) interminable

    (C) inaccessible

    (D) obsolete

    (E) illegible

15. Despite their outward resemblance, the brothers could not be more - - - - temperamentally; while one is quiet and circumspect, the other is brash and - - - - .

    (A) inimical .. timid

    (B) passionate .. superficial

    (C) dissimilar .. audacious

    (D) different .. forgiving

    (E) alike .. respectful

16. Her scholarly rigor and capacity for - - - - enabled her to undertake research projects that less - - - - people would have found too difficult and tedious.

    (A) fanaticism .. slothful

    (B) comprehension .. indolent

    (C) analysis .. careless

    (D) negligence .. dedicated

    (E) concentration .. disciplined

17. Even if - - - - life exists elsewhere in the universe, we humans may never know it, since it may be impossible for us to - - - - with these alien beings.

    (A) avaricious .. confer

    (B) prodigal .. reside

    (C) sentient .. communicate

    (D) lachrymose .. traipse

    (E) extraneous .. exit

# REMEMBER...

Sentence Completion questions are the Critical Reading section's most student-friendly question type.

Use Kaplan's Sentence Completion Attack Strategy:

- Read the sentence for clue words.
- Predict the answer.
- Select the best match.
- Plug your answer choice into the sentence.

Clue words help you predict how to fill in blanks.

End-of section questions can be figured out by:

- Avoiding tricky wrong answers
- Taking apart tough sentences
- Working around tough vocabulary

# ANSWERS AND EXPLANATIONS

## 1. C

This fairly easy sentence contains the clue word *and*. Since the phrase *dividing the consonants from the vowels* is joined to *writing each* with the word *and*, the two phrases must agree with each other. So, whatever goes in the blank must go along with the idea of dividing consonants and vowels. The choice that makes sense is (C) *separately*: The Greeks divided consonants from vowels and wrote each separately. The rest of the choices don't fit the context. For instance, (E) *accurately* might have seemed sensible, but the whole point is that the Greeks divided up their letters, not that they wrote precisely.

## 2. B

The clue here is the phrase *was smaller than he looked*. The missing word has to mean *made large*r or *made to seem larger*. Choice (B), *magnified*, is the answer. *Disparaged* (C) means belittled. *Admonished* (E) means scolded. In this question, (A) and (D) do not make sense in the context. The stranger's stature cannot be *worsened* because it was never suggested that it was bad in the first place, and a *disfigured* stature would cause alarm, not be caused by alarm.

## 3. A

The word *although* indicates contrast. The contrast is between the risk and the public's concern. Choice (A) is the only one that presents a clear contrast: the risk didn't decrease, but the public's concern did.

## 4. E

The phrase "warning both sides against encroachments on American interests" indicates that Wilson was attempting to prevent each side from taking an action that would force the United States to get involved in the war. Choice (E), *neutrality*, gets this point across. *Involvement* (A) suggests the opposite of the correct answer. *Belligerence* (B) is the quality of being warlike; *versatility* (C) means being able to handle a variety of different situations; *magnanimity* (D) is generosity.

## 5. C

You're specifically told that there's a contrast between the buildings and the subway stations. Checking the answer choices for a word that contrasts in meaning with "graceful curves," you find that the answer is (C), *angular*, which means "jagged" or "angled."

## 6. C

Don't give up if you don't know the word *feral*. Instead, read this two-blank sentence looking for one blank that leaps out as predictable. Start working with that one, and use it to rule out choices for the second blank.

If the second blank looks easier, start with that. You're told that *bird species were exterminated by cats*. These cats had something to do with *pets abandoned here decades ago by sailors*. That probably means the cats were (C) *descendants* of pets, but check out the other choices.

Since the pets were abandoned on the island decades ago, the cats couldn't logically be (B) *liberators* of pets, (D) *signals* of pets, or (E) *ancestors* of pets. And it's unlikely they'd be (A) *competitors* of pets, either. (C) makes the most sense in the second blank.

Now try the first blank. Bird species indigenous to the island were exterminated by the descendants of abandoned pets—that seems to make sense. A quick glance at the other choices confirms that (C) is right.

## 7. E

Your clue is *unfortunately*. The treasurer's plan unfortunately may not work because it - - - - gaining access to certain funds that may never become available. To fill the blank, look for a phrase like "relies on" or is "based on." The closest choice is (E) *hinges on*. The other four phrases don't make sense.

## 8. B

In the first blank, something factual is contrasted with conjecture; (B) *evidence* and (E) *documentation* are both possible answers. In the second blank, it doesn't make sense to say that something could (E) *inspire* previously held views, but something could certainly (B) *refute* previously held views, so (B) is the correct answer.

## 9. E

Gary must have been upset because his family heirlooms and personal mementos had been lost or destroyed in the fire. So look for a first word that means "upset" and a second word that means "loss." (A) *depressed*, (E) *distraught*, and (D) *mournful* work best for the first blank. Since *destruction* fits the second blank best, (E) is correct.

In (B), *eradication* is related to destruction but isn't usually applied to objects, such as personal mementos. Besides, Gary certainly wasn't *noncommittal* about the loss, so the first blank for (B) doesn't fit.

## 10. D

The major contrast in this sentence is one of gender: female authors versus masculine pen names. The second blank will almost certainly be filled by something like "masculine." The only choices whose second words have anything to do with masculine are (A) and (D). *Patriarchal* seems a bit overspecialized in this context, but check the first words to make sure that (D) male is the better choice.

*Pseudonyms* are used by people who don't want their work published under their real names. When you plug (A) and (D) into the sentence, (D) makes the internal logic tighter: The novels written by female authors were initially published under masculine pseudonyms because works by *male* authors generally received more favorable reviews.

## 11. E

An eruption that kills many thousands of people must be "bad" or "severe." (E), *disastrous*, is the obvious first word, though *fateful* or *blistering* is possible. (B) *inoffensive* is clearly wrong, and it doesn't make sense to describe a natural disaster as (C) *immoral*.

So now, for the second blank, check (A), (D), and (E). It makes no sense to say the eruption *diminished* or *authorized* havoc. (E) *wreaked* is the best answer.

## 12. D

The word *but* indicates contrast. If you plug in the answer choices, (D) makes the most sense with the word *imagination* and completes the contrast: the public became quickly excited about the issue, but agreement among experts as to the significance of the scrolls has been slower in coming. None of the other choices provides a clear contrast of ideas. In addition, *still* suggests a lack of understanding, so (A) and (C) cannot be correct.

## 13. C

The missing word describes people who starve themselves and become malnourished. Choice (C), *emaciated*, which means extremely thin, is the only choice that really fits. (A) and (E) are the exact opposites of what's needed, and *lachrymose* (B) means tearful. (D), *superfluous*, means unnecessary, which would be a comment on the person's social, not physical, status.

## 14. D

If new editions of this book are based on "more authoritative," or more accurate, manuscripts, previous editions would be rendered out-of-date, or *obsolete* (D)—scholars wouldn't use the old editions because the new ones are markedly superior. However, the new edition wouldn't render the old edition *incomprehensible* (A), *interminable* (B), *inaccessible* (C), or *illegible* (E).

## 15. C

The clue word *despite* indicates that the brothers must have different temperaments—making *dissimilar* (C) and *different* (D) both possibilities. The second word has to contrast with "quiet and *circumspect*," and be similar in tone to *"brash"*; *audacious,* or bold, is the only choice that makes sense, so (C) is correct.

## 16. E

It's easier to start with the second blank. You need a word that goes with *rigor* and contrasts with finding things "difficult and tedious." *Slothful* (A) and *indolent* (B) both mean lazy, so they're the opposite of what you need. Only *dedicated* (D) and *disciplined* (E) fit. Eliminate the other choices and try (D) and (E) in the first blank. The correct choice will be a quality held by a dedicated, rigorous scholar, so *concentration* (E) is the answer. *Negligence* (D) is the opposite of what you're looking for.

## 17. C

Assuming some alien intelligence exists, why might humans never know it? Logically, it must be because we can't (C) *communicate* with the alien life forms. (C) works: If *sentient*, or conscious, life exists, we humans might never know because we could be unable to *communicate* with that life. In (A), *confer* might be possible, but *avaricious* won't fit.

# Chapter Ten: **Build Your Vocabulary**

- **Diffusing Difficult Words**
- **Boosting Your Vocabulary**
- **Using Roots to Determine Meaning**

Both Critical Reading question types—Sentence Completion questions and Reading Comprehension questions—depend on your ability to work with unfamiliar words. You won't be asked to actually define any words on the SAT, but you will often need to have a sense of their meaning to answer both types of questions.

If you have only a week or two to prepare for the SAT (or you just can't take it anymore!), go straight to the "Decoding Strange Words on the Test" section of this chapter and master those skills. If you still have abundant time and energy, read on.

## TOUGH SAT WORDS

There are two types of tough SAT words:
- Unfamiliar words
- Familiar words with secondary meanings

Some words are hard because you haven't seen them before. The words *scintilla* or *circumlocution*, for instance, are probably not part of your everyday vocabulary, but they might pop up on your SAT.

Easy words, such as *recognize* or *appreciation*, can also trip you up on the test because they have secondary meanings that you aren't used to. Reading Comprehension questions, in particular, will throw you familiar words with unfamiliar meanings.

To get a sense of your vocabulary strength, we've provided a representative list of words you might find on the SAT. Take a couple of minutes to work through it and see how many you know. How many words can you define? Write your answer right in the book. Give yourself one point for each word you know. (The answers follow, so don't cheat by looking at them. As authority figures like to say: you'll only be hurting yourself.)

## KAPLAN'S VOCABULARY-BUILDING ATTACK STRATEGY

A great vocabulary can't be built overnight, but you can develop a better SAT vocabulary in a relatively short period of time with a minimum amount of pain. But you need to study wisely. Be strategic. How well you use your time between now and the day of the test is just as important as how much time you spend prepping.

Here's our three-step plan for building your vocabulary for the SAT:

- Learn words strategically.
- Use word families.
- Learn word roots and prefixes.

### Learn Words Strategically

The best words to learn are words that have appeared often on the SAT. The test makers are not very creative in their choice of words for each test, so words that have appeared frequently are likely bets to show up again.

A good resource for SAT vocabulary is our online flashcards. Don't forget to log on to kaptest.com/booksonline to practice your SAT vocabulary skills.

### SAT Word Roots

Most SAT words are made up of prefixes and roots that can get you at least partway to a definition. Often, that's all you need to get a right answer. Use the Root Word list at the end of this chapter to learn the most valuable SAT word roots. Target these words in your vocabulary review. Learn a few new roots a day, then familiarize yourself with meanings and sample words.

## Personalize Your Study Method

There's not just one *right* way to study vocabulary. Figure out a study method that works best for you, and stick to it. Here are some proven strategies:

- Use flashcards. Write down new words or word groups and run through them whenever you have a few spare minutes. Put one new word or word group on one side of a 3 x 5 index card and a short definition on the back.

- Make a vocabulary notebook. List words in one column and their meaning in another. Test yourself. Cover up the meanings, and see what words you can define from memory. Make a sample sentence using each word in context.

- Make a vocabulary tape. Record unknown words and their definitions. Pause for a moment before you read the definition. This will give you time to define the word in your head when you play the tape back. Quiz yourself. Listen to your tape in your portable cassette player. Play it in the car, on the bus, or whenever you have a few spare moments.

- Think of hooks that lodge a new word in your mind: Create visual images of words. For example, to remember the verb form of flag, you can picture a flag drooping or losing energy as the wind dies down.

- Use rhymes and other devices that help you remember the words. For example, you might remember that a *verbose* person uses a lot of verbs.

It doesn't matter which techniques you use, as long as you learn words steadily and methodically. Doing so over several months with regular reviews is ideal.

## DECODING STRANGE WORDS ON THE TEST

Trying to learn every word that could possibly appear on the SAT is like trying to memorize the license plate number of every car on the freeway. There are just too many to commit to memory.

No matter how much time you spend with flashcards, vocabulary tapes, or word lists, you're bound to face some mystery words on your SAT. No big deal. Just as you can use your basic multiplication skills to find the product of even the largest numbers, you can use what you know about words to focus on likely meanings of tough vocabulary words.

## Go With Your Hunches

When you look at an unfamiliar word, your first reaction may be to say, "Don't know it. Gotta skip it." Not so fast. Vocabulary knowledge on the SAT is not an all-or-nothing proposition.

- Some words you know so well you can rattle off a dictionary definition of them.
- Some words you "sort of" know. You understand them when you see them in context, but don't feel confident using them yourself.
- Some words are vaguely familiar. You know you've heard them somewhere before.

If you think you recognize a word, go with your hunch!

## Remember Where You've Heard the Word Before

If you can recall a phrase in which the word appears, that may be enough to eliminate some answer choices or even zero in on the right answer.

> Between the two villages was a —— through
> which passage was difficult and hazardous.

(A) precipice

(B) beachhead

(C) quagmire

(D) market

(E) prairie

To answer this question, you need to know whether or not to eliminate the word *quagmire*. You may remember *quagmire* from news reports referring to "a foreign policy *quagmire*" or "a *quagmire* of financial indebtedness." If you can remember how *quagmire* was used, you'll have a rough idea of what it means, and you'll see it fits. You may also be reminded of the word *mire*, as in "We got *mired* in the small details and never got to the larger issue." Sounds something like stuck, right? You don't need an exact definition. A *quagmire* is a situation that's difficult to get out of, so (C) is correct. Literally, a *quagmire* is a bog or swamp.

## Decide Whether the Word Has a Positive or Negative Charge

Simply knowing that you're dealing with a positive or negative word can earn you points on the SAT. For example, look at the word *cantankerous*. Say it to yourself. Can you guess whether it's positive or negative? Often words that sound harsh (such as *irk*) have a negative meaning, whereas smooth-sounding words (such as *benevolent*) tend to have positive meanings. If *cantankerous* sounded negative to you, you're right. It means *ill-tempered, disagreeable* or *difficult*.

You can also use prefixes and roots to help determine a word's charge. *Mal, de, dis, un, in, im, a,* and *mis* often indicate a negative, whereas *pro, ben,* and *magn* are often positives.

Not all SAT words sound positive or negative; some sound neutral. But if you can define the charge, you can probably eliminate some answer choices on that basis alone. Here's an example.

> He seemed at first to be honest and loyal, but
> before long it was necessary to --- him for his
> --- behavior.
>
> (A) admonish . . steadfast
> (B) extol . . conniving
> (C) reprimand . . scrupulous
> (D) exalt . . insidious
> (E) castigate . . perfidious

All you need to know to answer this question is that negative words are needed in both blanks. Then you can scan the answer choices for one that contains two clearly negative words. Even if you don't know what all the words mean, you can use your sense of positive or negative charge to eliminate answers. Choice (E) is right. *Castigate* means *punish* or *scold harshly*, and *perfidious* means *treacherous*.

## Use Your Foreign Language Skills

Many of the roots you'll encounter in SAT words come from Latin. Spanish, French, and Italian also come from Latin and have retained much of it in their modern forms. English is also a cousin to German and Greek. That means that if you don't recognize a word, try to remember if you know a similar word in another language. Look at the word *carnal*. Unfamiliar? What about *carne*, as in *chili con carne*? *Carn* means *meat* or *flesh*, which leads you straight to the meaning of *carnal*—pertaining to the flesh.

You could decode *carnivorous* (meat eating) in the same way. You can almost always figure out something about strange words on the test because SAT words are never all that strange. Chances are that few words on the SAT will be totally new to you, even if your recollection is more subliminal than vivid.

## When All Else Fails

If you feel totally at a loss, eliminate choices that are clearly wrong and make an educated guess from the remaining choices. A wrong answer won't hurt you much, but a right answer will help you a lot.

## REMEMBER...

There are two types of hard SAT words:

- Unfamiliar words
- Familiar words with secondary meanings

A great vocabulary can't be built overnight, but you can develop a better SAT vocabulary with a minimum of pain.

The best words to learn are words that have appeared often on the SAT. Find them at kaptest.com/booksonline.

Word families are groups of words with common meanings.

Most SAT words are made up of prefixes and roots that can get you at least partway to a definition. Learning word roots will help you with these words.

There are more ways to decode hard words when you are taking the test:

- Go with your hunch.
- Remember where you've heard the word before.
- Determine whether the word has a positive or negative charge
- Use your foreign language skills

## WORD ROOT LIST

If you don't have much time to spend on your vocabulary, skim through this Root List to familiarize yourself with the Latin and Greek roots of commonly tested SAT words.

**A, AN—not, without**
amoral, atrophy, asymmetrical, anarchy, anesthetic, anomaly

**AB, A—from, away, apart**
abdicate, aberration, abhor, abrogate, abscond, annul, aversion

**AC, ACR—sharp, sour**
acerbic, exacerbate, acute, acuity, acumen, acrid, acrimony

**AD, A—to, toward**
adhere, adjacent, adjunct, admonish, adroit, accede, aggrandize, ascribe, attest

**ALI, ALTR—another**
alias, alienate, inalienable, altruism

**AM, AMI—love**
amorous, amiable, amity

**AMBI, AMPHI—both**
ambiguous, ambivalent, ambidextrous, amphibious

**AMBL, AMBUL—walk**
amble, ambulatory, perambulator, somnambulist

**ANIM—mind, spirit, breath**
animal, animosity, unanimous, magnanimous

**ANN, ENN—year**
annual, annuity, superannuated, biennial, perennial

**ANTE, ANT—before**
antecedent, antediluvian, antebellum, anterior, antiquated

**ANTHROP—human**
anthropomorphic, misanthrope

**ANTI, ANT—against, opposite**
antidote, antipathy, antithesis, antagonist, antonym

**AUD—hear**
audio, audience, audition, audible

**AUTO—self**
autocrat, autonomous

**BELLI, BELL—war**
belligerent, bellicose, antebellum

**BENE, BEN—good**
benevolent, benefactor, beneficent, benign

**BI—two**
bisect, bilateral, bilingual, biped

**BIO—life**
biology, amphibious, symbiotic

CAD, CAS, CID—happen, fall
accident, cadence, cascade

CAP, CIP—head
captain, capitulate, precipitous, precipitate

CARN—flesh
carnage, carnivorous, incarnate

CAP, CAPT, CEPT, CIP—take, hold, seize
capacious, captivate, intercept, inception, anticipate, emancipation

CEDE, CESS—yield, go
cessation, incessant, precede, antecedent, intercede, secede

CHROM—color
chrome, chromatic, monochrome

CHRON—time
chronology, chronic, anachronism

CIRCUM—around
circumference, circumlocution, circumscribe, circumspect

CLIN, CLIV—slope
incline, declivity, proclivity

CLUD, CLUS, CLAUS, CLOIS—shut, close
conclude, reclusive, claustrophobia, cloister

CO, COM, CON—with, together
coalesce, coerce, cogent, colloquial, complacent, compliant, compunction, conciliatory, conjure, consensus

COGN, GNO—know
recognize, cognition, diagnosis, agnostic, prognosis, ignorant

CONTRA—against
incontrovertible, contravene

CORP—body
corpse, corporeal, corpulence

COSMO, COSM—world
cosmos, microcosm

CRAC, CRAT—rule, power
democracy, bureaucracy, aristocratic, technocrat

CRED—trust, believe
incredible, credulous, credence

CRESC, CRET—grow
crescent, crescendo, accretion

CULP—blame, fault
culprit, culpable, inculpate

CURR, CURS—run
current, concur, cursory, precursor, incursion

DE—down, out, apart
debilitate, declivity, defunct, deprecate, deride

DEC—ten, tenth
decade, decimal, decimate

DEMO, DEM—people
democrat, demographics, demagogue, epidemic

DI, DIURN—day
diary, quotidian, diurnal

DIA—across
diagonal, diatribe, diaphanous

DIC, DICT—speak
abdicate, diction, interdict

DIS, DIF, DI—not, apart, away
discordant, discursive, disparate, diffidence, diffuse, digress, divert

DOC, DOCT—teach
docile, doctrine

DOL—pain
condolence, doleful, dolorous, indolent

DUC, DUCT—lead
induce, conduct, viaduct, induct

EGO—self
egoist, egocentric

EN, EM—in, into
enter, entice, encumber, endemic, embellish, embroil, empathy

ERR—wander
erratic, aberration, errant

EU—well, good
eulogy, euphemism, euphony

EX, E—out, out of
exacerbate, exculpate, exorbitant, expedient, expurgate, extenuate, extricate, evoke, elicit, egress

FAC, FIC, FECT, FY, FEA—make, do
factory, facility, benefactor, fictive, beneficent, affect, feasible

FAL, FALS—deceive
infallible, fallacious, false

FERV—boil
fervent, fervid, effervescent

FID—faith, trust
confident, diffidence, perfidious

FLU, FLUX—flow
affluent, confluence, flux

FORE—before
forecast, foreboding, forestall

FRAG, FRAC—break
fragment, fracture, diffract, fractious, refract

FUS—pour
profuse, infusion, effusive, diffuse

GEN—birth, class, kin
generation, homogeneous, ingenious, progeny

GRAD, GRESS—step
retrograde, centigrade, gradient, digress, transgress

GRAPH, GRAM—writing
biography, bibliography, epigraph, grammar, epigram

GRAT—pleasing
grateful, gratitude, ingrate, congratulate, gratuitous

GRAV, GRIEV—heavy
aggravate, aggrieve, grievous

GREG—crowd, flock
segregate, gregarious, egregious

HABIT, HIBIT—have, hold
cohabit, habitat, inhibit

HAP—by chance
haphazard, hapless, mishap

HELIO, HELI—sun
heliocentric, heliotrope, aphelion, perihelion

HETERO—other
heterogeneous, heterodox

HOL—whole
holocaust, holistic

HOMO—same
homogeneous, homonym

HOMO—man
homo sapiens, bonhomie

HYDR—water
hydrant, dehydration

HYPER—too much, excess
hyperactive, hyperbole

HYPO—too little, under
hypothesis, hypothetical

IN, IG, IL, IM, IR—not
incorrigible, indefatigable,
inexorable, ignorant, ignoble,
illicit, illimitable, impasse,
impecunious, irregular

IN, IL, IM, IR—in, on, into
incandescent, ingratiate, introvert,
illustrate, imbue, immerse,
irrigate, irritate

INTER—between, among
intercede, intercept, interdiction,
interject, interlocutor, interloper

INTRA, INTR—within
intrastate, intravenous, intrinsic

IT, ITER—between, among
transit, itinerant, transitory

JECT, JET—throw
interject, trajectory, jettison

JOUR—day
journal, adjourn, sojourn

JUD—judge
judicious, adjudicate

JUNCT, JUG—join
adjunct, injunction, subjugate

JUR—swear, law
adjure, conjure, perjure

LAT—side
lateral, collateral, unilateral

LAV, LAU, LU—wash
lavatory, laundry, ablution

LEG, LEC, LEX—read, speak
legible, lecture, lexicon

LEV—light
elevate, levitate, levity, alleviate

LIBER—free
liberty, liberal, libertarian, libertine

LIG, LECT—choose, gather
eligible, elect, select

LIG, LI, LY—bind
ligament, liable, liaison, ally

LING, LANG—tongue
lingo, language, linguistics

LITER—letter
literate, alliteration, literal

LITH—stone
monolith, lithograph, megalith

LOQU, LOC, LOG—speech, thought
loquacious, colloquy,
circumlocution, interlocutor,
philology, neologism

LUC, LUM—light
lucid, elucidate, pellucid,
translucent, illuminate

LUD, LUS—play
ludicrous, allude, delusion,
allusion, illusory

MACRO—great
macrocosm, macrobiotics

MAG, MAJ, MAS, MAX—great
magnanimous, magnate,
magnitude, majesty, master,
maximum

MAL—bad
malady, maladroit, malevolent

MAN—hand
manual, emancipate, manifest

MAR—sea
submarine, marine, maritime

MATER, MATR—mother
maternal, matron, matrilineal

MEDI—middle
intermediary, medieval, mediate

MEGA—great
megalomania, megaton, megalith

MEM, MIN—remember
memento, reminisce

METER, METR, MENS—measure
meter, thermometer, perimeter,
metronome, commensurate

MICRO—small
microorganism, microcosm

MIS—wrong, bad, hate
misanthrope, misapprehension

MIT, MISS—send
transmit, emit, missive

MOLL—soft
mollify, emollient

MON, MONIT—warn
admonish, monitor, premonition

MONO—one
monologue, monotonous

MOR—custom, manner
moral, mores, morose

MOR, MORT—dead
moribund, mortal, amortize

MORPH—shape
amorphous, metamorphosis

MOV, MOT, MOB, MOM—move
remove, motion, mobile,
momentous

MUT—change
mutate, mutability, immutable

NAT, NASC—born
neonate, innate, nascent

NAU, NAV—ship, sailor
nautical, circumnavigate

NEG—not, deny
negative, abnegate, renege

NEO—new
neoclassical, neophyte

NIHIL—none, nothing
annihilation, nihilism

NOM, NYM—name
nomenclature, misnomer,
ignominious, anonymity

NOX, NIC, NEC, NOC—harm
obnoxious, noxious, pernicious,
internecine, innocuous

NOV—new
novelty, innovation, novitiate

NUMER—number
innumerable, enumerate

OB—against
obdurate, obsequious, obstinate,
obstreperous

OMNI—all
omnipresent, omnipotent, omniscient, omnivorous

ONER—burden
onerous, exonerate

OPER—work
operate, cooperate, inoperable

PAC—peace
pacify, pacifist, pacific

PALP—feel
palpable, palpitation

PAN—all
panacea, panegyric, panoply

PATER, PATR—father
paternal, expatriate, patrician

PATH, PASS—feel, suffer
sympathy, antipathy, empathy, apathy, pathos, impassioned

PEC—money
pecuniary, impecunious, peculation

PED, POD—foot
pedestrian, pediment, expedient, biped, tripod

PEL, PULS—drive
compel, expel, propel, compulsion

PEN—almost
peninsula, penultimate, penumbra

PEND, PENS—hang
pendulous, compendium, suspense, propensity

PER—through, by, for, throughout
percipient, perfunctory, perusal, perennial, peregrinate

PER—against, destruction
perfidious, pernicious, perjure

PERI—around
perimeter, periphery, perihelion, peripatetic

PET—seek, go toward
impetus, impetuous, petulant

PHIL—love
philosopher, philanthropy, bibliophile

PHOB—fear
phobia, xenophobia

PHON—sound
phonograph, euphony, phonetics, phonics

PLAC—calm, please
placate, implacable, placid, complacent

PON, POS—put, place
proponent, posit, juxtaposition, depose

PORT—carry
portable, deportment, rapport

POT—drink
potion, potable

POT—power
potential, potent, potentate, omnipotence

PRE—before
precede, preclude, precocious, precursor, predilection, prescient

PRIM, PRI—first
primeval, primordial, pristine

PRO—ahead, forth
proclivity, promontory, proscribe

PROTO—first
prototype, protagonist, protocol

PROX, PROP—near
approximate, propinquity, proximity

PSEUDO—false
pseudoscientific, pseudonym

PYR—fire
pyre, pyrotechnics, pyromania

QUAD, QUAR, QUAT—four
quadrant, quarantine, quaternary

QUES, QUER, QUIS, QUIR—
question
inquest, query, querulous,
inquisitive, inquiry

QUIE—quiet
disquiet, acquiesce, quiescent,
requiem

QUINT, QUIN—five
quintuplets, quintessence

RADI, RAMI—branch
radius, radiate, radiant, eradicate,
ramification

RECT, REG—straight, rule
rectitude, rectify, regular

REG—king, rule
regal, regent, interregnum

RETRO—backward
retrospective, retroactive

RID, RIS—laugh
ridiculous, deride, derision

ROG—ask
interrogate, derogatory, abrogate

RUD—rough, crude
rude, erudite, rudimentary

RUPT—break
disrupt, interrupt, rupture

SACR, SANCT—holy
sacred, sanctify, sanction

SCRIB, SCRIPT, SCRIV—write
ascribe, circumscribe, inscribe,
proscribe, script, manuscript

SE—apart, away
segregate, secede, sedition

SEC, SECT, SEG—cut
secant, sector, dissect, bisect,
intersect, segment

SED, SID—sit
sedate, sedentary, supersede,
residence, assiduous, insidious

SEM—seed, sow
seminar, seminal, disseminate

SEN—old
senior, senile, senescent

SENT, SENS—feel, think
sentiment, sentient, assent,
consensus, nonsense

SEQU, SECU—follow
sequence, obsequious,
non sequitur, consecutive

SIM, SEM—similar, same
verisimilitude, semblance,
dissemble

SIGN—mark, sign
signal, designation, assignation

SIN—curve
sinuous, insinuate

SOL—sun
solar, parasol, solarium, solstice

SOL—alone
solo, solitude, soliloquy, solipsism

SOMN—sleep
somnolent, somnambulist

SON—sound
sonic, sonorous, resonate

SOPH—wisdom
philosopher, sophisticated

SPEC, SPIC—see, look
circumspect, retrospective, perspicacious, perspicuous

SPER—hope
prosper, prosperous, despair

SPERS, SPAR—scatter
sparse, aspersion, disparate

SPIR—breathe
respire, inspire, aspire, transpire

STRICT, STRING—bind
strict, stricture, constrict, stringent

STRUCT, STRU—build
structure, obstruct, construe

SUB—under
subjugate, subliminal, subvert

SUMM—highest
summit, summary, consummate

SUPER, SUR—above
supervise, supersede, superfluous, insurmountable, surfeit

SURGE, SURRECT—rise
resurgent, insurrection

SYN, SYM—together
synthesis, syncopation, symposium, symbiosis

TACIT, TIC—silent
tacit, taciturn, reticent

TACT, TAG, TANG—touch
tactile, contagious, tangent, tangential, tangible

TEN, TIN, TAIN—hold, twist
detention, tenable, tenacious, pertinacious, retinue, retain

TEND, TENS, TENT—stretch
intend, tension, tensile, ostensible, contentious

TERM—end
terminal, terminus, interminable

TERR—earth, land
terrain, terrestrial, subterranean

TEST—witness
attest, testimonial, protestation

THERM—heat
thermometer, thermal

TIM—fear, frightened
timid, intimidate, timorous

TOP—place
topic, topography, utopia

TORT—twist
distort, extort, tortuous

TORP—stiff, numb
torpedo, torpid, torpor

TOX—poison
toxic, toxin

TRACT—draw
tractor, intractable, protract

TRANS—across, over, through
transport, transgress, transient

TREM, TREP—shake
tremulous, trepidation, intrepid

TURB—shake
disturb, turbulent, perturbation

UMBR—shadow
umbrage, adumbrate, penumbra

UNI, UN—one
unify, unilateral, unanimous

URB—city
urban, suburban, urbane

VAC—empty
vacant, evacuate, vacuous

VAL, VAIL—value, strength
valid, ambivalent, convalescence, prevail

VEN, VENT—come
convene, contravene, intervene, venue, circumvent, advent

VER—true
verity, veracious, verdict

VERB—word
verbose, verbiage, verbatim

VERT, VERS—turn
revert, incontrovertible, versatile, aversion

VICT, VINC—conquer
victory, evict, evince, invincible

VID, VIS—see
evident, vision, visage, supervise

VIL—base, mean
vile, vilify, revile

VIV, VIT—life
vivid, vital, convivial, vivacious

VOC, VOK, VOW—call, voice
vocal, equivocate, vociferous, convoke, evoke, invoke, avow

VOL—wish
malevolent, benevolent, volition

VOLV, VOLUT—turn, roll
revolve, evolve, convoluted

VOR—eat
carnivore, voracious

# What's the best way to prepare for the New SAT?

## *Create a study group!*

### Kaplan will even throw in a free* pizza party to help you get started.

*How does the Kaplan NEW SAT Study Group Pizza Party work?*

1. Purchase Kaplan's *The NEW SAT 2005* or Kaplan's *The NEW SAT 2005 with CD-ROM*, both of which include a Kaplan NEW SAT study group guide. Save your receipt as proof of purchase.

2. Fully complete the official request form below.

3. Mail the fully completed official request form plus your original receipt for Kaplan's *The NEW SAT 2005* or Kaplan's *The NEW SAT 2005 with CD-ROM* as proof of purchase to: Kaplan/Simon & Schuster, 12th Floor, 1230 Avenue of the Americas, New York, NY 10020.

4. Kaplan will send you a gift certificate for a free Domino's large one-topping pizza and a 2-liter bottle of Coke® to use at one of your NEW SAT study group meetings.

*Get a gift certificate† for a free Domino's large one-topping pizza and a 2-liter bottle of Coke® when you submit your original receipt for Kaplan's *The NEW SAT 2005* or Kaplan's *The NEW SAT 2005 with CD-ROM* as proof of purchase and the fully completed official request form below. Please allow 10-12 weeks for delivery. Delivery cannot be guaranteed unless you include your zip code on the official request form. The Kaplan NEW SAT Study Group Pizza Party is valid in the U.S. (void in Puerto Rico) and Canada (void in Quebec) while supplies last. Offer may not be combined with any other offer. All Domino's Pizza® terms and conditions apply. Void where prohibited or otherwise restricted by law. All submissions become the property of Simon & Schuster and will not be returned. Simon & Schuster is not responsible for lost, late, illegible, incomplete, postage-due or misdirected forms or mail. Requests not complying with all offer requirements will not be honored. Approximate retail value of Kaplan NEW SAT Study Group Pizza Party is $14.00. Offer ends the earlier of January 12, 2005 or while supplies last. All request forms must be received no later than January 12, 2005.

†Domino's Pizza® gift certificate valid at participating locations only. For a store near you, visit www.dominos.com.

------------------------------------------------------------

## Kaplan NEW SAT Study Group Pizza Party Official Request Form

I am enclosing my sales receipt of Kaplan's *The NEW SAT 2005* or Kaplan's *The NEW SAT 2005 with CD-ROM* as proof of purchase. Please send me my gift certificate for a free Domino's large one-topping pizza and a 2-liter bottle of Coke® for my Kaplan NEW SAT Study Group Pizza Party.

Name _____

Address _____

City _____ State _____ Zip _____